Praise for

Kick Ass Social Commerce for E-preneurs

"When it comes to who reigns supreme in Social Commerce, John Lawson is a legend! In this book, John shows you how to leverage Social Media and make it a potent, highly effective, and efficient lever to grow your business. You want easy? Go talk to your shrink. You want to make money on the Internet? Buy this book!"

—*Paul Greenberg, Cofounder of DealsDirect and CEO of the Australian National Online Retailers Association*

"John Lawson is a Master Internet Marketer and Social Commerce expert who sells millions of dollars' worth of products online and then liberally shares his hard-earned knowledge with us. He is funny, impassioned, and most important, INFORMATIVE! This book is a MUST read to GROW your business."

—*Ramon Ray, Editor and Technology Evangelist, Smallbiztechnology.com*

"John Lawson is a natural communicator, a visionary, and someone that practices what he preaches! Debra Schepp is an outstanding writer who has been at the coalface of eCommerce for over ten years. John Lawson + Debra Schepp = a winning recipe for Kick Ass results!"

—*Phil Leahy, Managing Director PeSA Internet Conference & Online Market Experts*

"If you're looking to get more Twitter followers or Facebook friends, there are an endless number of books covering that well-trodden ground. But if you're looking for a deeper understanding of how social, mobile, and cloud technologies are creating opportunities to build powerful new eCommerce business models, then this is the book for you! Get it, read it, live it, and enjoy it. Then go out and kick some ass."

—*Brent Leary, Partner at CRM Essentials*

"John Lawson isn't just talking about it . . . he's doing it! He's in the day-to-day retail trenches just like us! When the Internet landscape has completely changed and Facebook has gone the way of MySpace, you'll already be optimizing your presence on The Next Big Thing because of the foundation you got from John's lessons."

—*Hillary DePiano, TheWhineSeller.com*

"Social media doesn't care how rich or pretty; short or tall; big or small you might be. It only responds to how interesting and interested you are. It levels the business playing field for everyone. John Lawson shows you how to win your customers' hearts, mindshare, and loyalty. His book gives you the skills that will make your cash register sing Ka-Ching!"

—*Shirley Tan, Author of* Ecom Hell

"There are books about Social Media, and then there are books about Social Media for eCommerce. If you want to get 'Likes, Followers, and Friends,' buy a book about getting 'Likes, Followers, and Friends.' But if you want to use Social Media to boost sales, increase profits, and engage your customers, then this is the book for you!"

—*Chris Green, Director, ScanPower.com*

"John Lawson knows how to use Social Media to build an engaged community that wants to buy products. Too many are out there telling unaware entrepreneurs that garnering 'Likes' and 'Followers' will grow their bottom line. Social Commerce is more than just a buzzword, and John does a great job of breaking down this complicated concept into bite-size chunks that are easy to comprehend. Are you ready to Kick Ass?"

—*Rick Backus, Cofounder & CEO of CPC Strategy*

"In the over-hyped world of social-anything, John Lawson is delivering the dream that others are trying to sell. 'Likes' and 'Followers' only count when you receive hard cash. John is showing us how!"

—*Bjorn Espenes, CEO and Founder of Finch LLC*

"I've known Debra Schepp for ten years now, and we've certainly shared plenty about eCommerce over those years. What makes Deb unique is her ability to find the topics and trends that really help people help themselves. Selling widgets on the Internet isn't rocket science, but there sure are plenty of people in the industry who try to convince you otherwise —and take all your hard-earned money in the process! Deb's ability to network and find the people who simplify things, then process their personal stories and connect them to the topics of the day, and then deliver that information so that it's accessible to people regardless of background or experience is second to none. There's a big difference between presenting oneself as an authority and being an authority. Few do both with grace and kindness. Deb delivers, and then some."

—*Andy Mowery, Cofounder of debnroo, inc.*

KICK ASS
SOCIAL
COMMERCE FOR
E-PRENEURS

KICK ASS SOCIAL COMMERCE FOR E-PRENEURS

IT'S NOT ABOUT LIKES— IT'S ABOUT SALES

BY **JOHN LAWSON**

WITH **DEBRA SCHEPP**

BenBella Books
Dallas, Texas

BenBella Books, Inc.
10300 N. Central Expressway, Suite #530
Dallas, TX 75231
www.benbellabooks.com

Send feedback to feedback@benbellabooks.com.

Printed in the United States of America
10 9 8 7 6 5 4 3 2 1

Library of Congress Cataloging-in-Publication Data

Lawson, John, 1965–
    Kick ass social commerce for e-preneurs : it's not about likes ... it's about sales /
John Lawson, with Debra Schepp.
        pages cm
    Includes bibliographical references and index.
        ISBN 978-1-939529-44-2 (pbk.) — ISBN 978-1-939529-45-9 (electronic)
    1. Electronic commerce—Social aspects. 2. Marketing—Social aspects.
    3. Internet marketing—Social aspects.   I. Schepp, Debra.   II. Title.
        HF5548.32.L387 2014
        658.8'72—dc23

                                                                    2013036472

Editing by Erin Kelley
Copyediting by Francesca Drago
Proofreading by Greg Teague and Rainbow Graphics, Inc.
Indexing by Clive Pyne, Book Indexing Services
Cover design by Rob Johnson
Text design and composition by Publishers' Design and Production Services, Inc.
Printed by Bang Printing

Distributed by Perseus Distribution
www.perseusdistribution.com

To place orders through Perseus Distribution:
Tel: (800) 343-4499
Fax: (800) 351-5073
E-mail: orderentry@perseusbooks.com

Significant discounts for bulk sales are available. Please contact Glenn Yeffeth at glenn@benbellabooks.com or (214) 750-3628.

This book is dedicated to my mommy, Dolores Lawson. I hope I make you proud ... Kiss. Eternal thanks to my partner, JD, whom I love dearly.

—JL

This one is for my husband, Brad, the coauthor of my life, and for my "sister" Ellen, who already loved me when I met him.

—DS

Contents

Contents

Foreword

H e started with the words, *"Entrepreneurship changed my life!"* and with that phrase, the force of nature known as John "ColderICE" Lawson began to mesmerize the audience of movers and shakers that had gathered from across the United States and Canada for the 2011 Small Business Influencer of the Year Awards in New York City.

He told of being a high school drop out from the projects in Queens, raised by a single mother who believed in him and supported him in everything he did. He talked about several false starts in his career and his beginnings in the IT field. But most of all, the audience was enthralled by this gentle giant with a heart of gold who spoke with passion and conviction about founding and running his multimillion dollar eCommerce business, 3rd Power Outlet.

In the next incarnation of his life, John remade himself into an internationally known speaker and published author, whose sole motivation is to give back to other entrepreneurs through sharing his insights, expertise, and experiences. Out of all the remarks made that evening, John's are the ones I remember the most.

As cofounder of the Small Business Influencer Awards and publisher of Small Business Trends and BizSugar.com, I am continually charged with the task of interviewing experts. Between reading hundreds of magazine, newspaper, and online articles that are written by and about business and internet specialists and personally speaking with hundreds more, I've become pretty good at identifying an authentic voice that is backed up by real life experiences.

John's remarks stuck in my mind because they exemplify the power of lessons learned through real-life doing.

John's knowledge doesn't come from schools. Everything he knows—and he knows a lot—comes from rolling up his sleeves and working in the trenches and doing the hard work. John is totally, completely about real life experiences.

And his real life experiences in social media and internet marketing are exactly what you will find in *Kick Ass Social Commerce for E-preneurs*. This is a book about carving out success online. This book is for the doers of the world.

Today, the world moves at fast pace. And if you are a serious entrepreneur, you don't have time for abstract theory and grand concepts. Entrepreneurs jump in where others fear to tread. We hustle. We climb over obstacles. We go around them. We ignore them.

We get stuff done.

So if you want to learn how to better navigate your success path in the world, you're going to want to learn from someone who is like you—someone who has overcome great odds; someone who forges ahead based on intuition; someone with street smarts and experience.

I love the way *Kick Ass* distills social media and online commerce down into timeless business concepts. The section in the book called "Everything Old Is New Again" perfectly illustrates this. In it, John helps you relate the concept of cold calling to the world of social media and online commerce. The way he describes it is so simple that it is genius!

As you read this book, you will get solid grounding and have at least a few "Aha! moments" as you pick up pointers that help you frame social media and integrate it into your business.

Now let me offer a piece of advice.

Words have power and positive words have positive power. So, I want you to pay close attention to the end of each chapter where you will find a summary called "That's a Rap!"

These are phrased in the form of action items and positive affirmations. An example comes at the end of the section on video, where he concludes with statements such as "I will focus on my video's content more than on its production. I already own enough equipment to get started."

You see, this book is all about helping you take the plunge and seize success TODAY. It's not about waiting until the planets align perfectly. Yes, you want to take enough time to understand how to do it the right way. But the most important thing is to take informed action. That's what entrepreneurs do—take action.

Now go read the book! Then get out there and grab success for yourself!

—*Anita Campbell, CEO and Publisher of Small Business Trends*

Introduction

In the Beginning, Man Created Intros . . .

Today is a beautiful spring day here in Atlanta, Georgia, and I am outside playing with my niece, Deva. She and I are having a ball with our new bottle of Super Bubble. I am the bubble manufacturer and she is the bubble destroyer, meaning that I blow them and she chases them and pops them. I will occasionally, however, grab one out of the air and catch it on my bubble wand. Each time I manage to catch one out of the air, my niece stares at me in fascination. (Yes, I know this is a business book, but trust me, this is going somewhere.)

She has the look of wonder when I catch the bubbles, like I am a master of bubbleology. Then the phone rings, so I quickly hand her the giant bottle of bubbles and the wand and make my way up on the porch. I sit down in the rocker on the porch to take the call. I watch Deva now both blowing and chasing her own self-made bubbles.

She dips the wand in the jar and blows. A stream of bubbles flows forth, but now comes the hard part for her. If she wants to be the bubble master like her uncle, she has to chase down the dispersed bubbles and navigate the wand under one so it will land perfectly. Unfortunately, at her age, it is a challenge, but she is very determined to make it happen.

Deva is blowing the bubbles just fine, but once the bubbles start to fly away, she begins to chase them and forgets that she is holding the bubble bottle. So she runs after the bubbles, letting the solution spill all over the yard. Then she begins the process over again: dip, blow, chase, spill. After four repetitions comes the realization that she's now out of bubble solution. Now the wand doesn't work, and she can't make or attempt to catch bubbles. Game over! Before the tears can begin, I come to the rescue with a bottle of dishwashing soap. Uncle Johnny saves the day!

Sometimes people can act like Deva with their businesses, too. They get so focused on the new bubble, and they start to chase it. What they fail to realize is that the bubble is only the byproduct of soap, water, and a puff of air. Deva was unable to discern that what I did had very little chasing involved. I waited for the right bubble to come down and land on the wand. I waited for the best bubble that was close and coming my way before catching it. I basically never left my spot to catch all of my bubbles!

Social media is the new bubble. Blow hard, and you've got Facebook. Blow again, poof, Twitter. One more time, and you've got LinkedIn, Pinterest, Instagram, etc. You get my drift. We see these pretty bubbles, and we run to chase them. But the entire time we're running, we are spilling the bubble solution all over the yard. We are chasing the new and shiny objects, giving little regard to what makes it all possible ... the bubble solution!

This book is the key to the mystery of social media. I guarantee that after reading just a chapter or two, you will *never* think the same way about social marketing for social commerce. You will know not only how to catch the bubbles, but you will know the formula for making more bubble solution. So no matter what bubbles come out today or in the future, you will know the chemical makeup for success.

There are thirteen chapters in this book, and they are broken down into two distinct parts. Part One is "the Meat." It's the system, the "how it all works" for social commerce. Part Two is "the Gravy." It is the application of the formula across the range of social networks. We wrote this book so you could move from theory to immediate action!

Do you know what the difference is between knowledge and wisdom? A real smart man once told me that to read a book is to gain knowledge, and to use what you learned in that book successfully is to gain wisdom: *huge* difference. I know lots of people who are much smarter than me in terms of book smarts. Matter of fact, most of them work with me as clients and some actually work for me as employees. They've got the book smarts. They have the knowledge. They can research a topic to death. They can write dissertations and speak in boardrooms or on stages. These guys and gals are smart as hell! But more often than not, when you tap them on the shoulder and ask, "So how much of that have you applied to your own work?" I hear crickets. They've done nothing. This is not a bad thing. It's just not who they are or how they operate. I am the opposite. I was born an entrepreneur. I was not trained in the best schools, with the alphabet soup behind my name. Matter of fact, the only letters I actually qualify for are HSD (high school dropout).

Yeah, I'm the guy who dropped out of high school, but who today has 117,349 feedbacks on eBay, where I've achieved Platinum PowerSeller status and completed more than 267,000 online transactions on the web

To put it plainly, I am *not* the smartest guy in the room, but I am full of the applied knowledge my coauthor and I will share in the following pages.

When I was beginning with social media and blogging, I wanted my own name, just like most people do. But when I did a search for John Lawson, more than 3.4 million people were listed on Google. I knew it would be way too hard for me to rank high enough to get noticed with that many folks sharing my name.

So I came up with a handle. I went through a lot of names while trying to settle on the perfect one. Then one day an old story came back to me …

Back in the segregated South, African Americans were not allowed to shop in the stores downtown that were for "Whites Only." So there was a vast black economy that consisted of black-owned shops and stores. When segregation was ended, many of these store owners suffered as blacks who were once banned from the stores in the city were now able to shop downtown. These black store owners would watch out of their storefronts and see the people walking past their shops to go and purchase the same items in town. From this there arose a saying among these retailers that "the White Man's ice was colder," and this was my inspiration for how I came up with ColderICE. I did a Google search on the phrase "ColderICE" back then, and there were fewer than three hundred results. I *knew* that with only three hundred results, I could be on the first page of Google search results in no time.

Well, that was it, I created my online presence by signing up for Twitter, and I used that handle instead of my name, which would have been JohnLawson34847 or some dumb name like that, and I just was not feeling it. So that is when ColderICE was born. Fast-forward to today and go to Google and type in "ColderICE" (in quotes, one word, no spaces). I just got back 54,700 results … And guess what? They are *all* mine. But the twist gets even better. I have parlayed that social influence so much that now, if you look up John Lawson on Google, I show up on the *first page* of more than 85 million results! That was when I realized the power of social media for anything I wanted to do. I am a commerce guy, so I want that power for commerce ... hence the subject matter of this book: social commerce. Let's make this money!

Let's discuss a couple of notes about how to read this book. Like I said, it is in two parts. Read *all* of Part One in its entirety—no cheating or skipping pages. All of the principles are laid out here. Once you do that, you can move to Part Two, where you can cherry-pick if you want to. No matter what, be sure to read the WordPress and Facebook chapters first.

There are a couple of reading aids we used to highlight some important stuff, too. We have ICE Breakers. They are there to shatter the myths you may have heard, so pay special attention to these features.

We also have our ICE Makers. These are action items. It's time to convert knowledge to wisdom and apply it in your own life. That is what the ICE Makers are for.

We have some extra author bonus content that has been prepared for you, and it is available on the book's website. You can access the bonus content at http://www.kickasssocialcommerce .com/bonus.

—John Lawson (Twitter: @ColderICE)
—Debra Schepp (Twitter: @DebSchepp)

PART ONE

The Meat–Social Commerce and King Consumers

CHAPTER 1

Don't Get It Twisted, Business Is Always Social

"You only live once! Get Busy!"

—*Sean "Diddy" Combs*

Welcome to the age-old world of social commerce! What? Were you expecting that I was going to tell you that social commerce was a startling, fascinating, frenetic, and *new* way of selling products? If that's what you were thinking, I suggest you fasten your seatbelts, now, and pull them tight. Social commerce is ancient! I would not be surprised if soon after the caveman invented the first chisel, he looked around for someone he could trade one with. *Look at this amazing new thing to carve with. I'll trade you one for some of those nuts and berries!* Well, maybe their language wasn't so clear, but people have been socially interacting around the exchange of goods almost as long as people have been on Earth.

No matter where you go in the world today, and I go all over the place, the one thing you can find, no matter where you are, is a central market area of some sort. Okay, so in first-world countries, that's likely a mall or a city center filled with expensive and elegant stores. But travel to developing countries, and you're still going to find a physical marketplace. Humans need commodities, and the ones who shop for those commodities need merchants to sell them. Not only that, but the people who make or sell one type of commodity still need many other types of things, too. So whether they come with coins, credit cards, or goods for bartering, people are going to interact with other people to exchange their currency or goods for the products and services they need. So, let's get it right from the beginning: Social commerce is as old as humanity.

Now, I won't disagree that the ways we interact to exchange goods and services have changed. That is very true. But the changes, dramatic as they seem within the last ten years, have actually been happening all along. Let's take a look at a relatively recent change that reverberates throughout our marketplace even today. I'm not talking about Facebook or Twitter.

AN UNLIKELY MILLIONAIRE

Sarah Breedlove was born on December 23, 1867 in Delta, Louisiana. She didn't begin life with all of the advantages a child should have. The Civil War was still a fresh wound for our country. When she arrived, her state was barely limping back from devastating years of war, and she was born African American in a time when such a respectful term for black Americans hadn't even been invented. And life didn't get easier for Sarah. She was orphaned at the age of seven, married off at the age of fourteen, and had her first child by the time she was seventeen. By the time she turned twenty, she was a widow. That is a lot to handle when, by today's standards, she would just be getting ready to set out on her own.

Like many African-American women of her time Sarah used a process to straighten her hair. Unfortunately the "process" included huge quantities of lye—an extremely harsh chemical used in soaps of the time. It did straighten hair, but it could also cause it to fall out! On top of everything else, Sarah was losing her hair, and she wasn't happy about it. One evening she decided to come up with a better type of hair treatment, hoping it would restore her hair. She mixed up an ointment in her bathtub and began applying it to her scalp. As she continued to use it instead of lye, she noticed that not only did her remaining hair look healthier, but also new hair had begun to cover her scalp in the sparse places! That's when she got a great idea and became what we would call today an "accidental entrepreneur." She never set out to build a business, let alone an empire, but she knew she wasn't the only woman having trouble with her hair treatments. Maybe some of her neighbors would be interested in her new ointment, too.

That's when Sarah Breedlove became Madame C. J. Walker, the woman who would go on to become America's first self-made female millionaire! But, that's getting ahead of the story. I just like stories to have happy endings, so I put it out there right now.

Sarah began small. She went door-to-door in her area, talking to other women about her new ointment. She found her neighbors, accustomed as they were to the old ways, skeptical of her newfangled product. So, she started giving demonstrations of her ointment right there in her prospective customers' kitchens. The ointment was a hit! It became so popular, and the demand for it increased so quickly, that she just couldn't keep up with production, marketing, sales, and distribution through her door-to-door business model of one person. Plus her customer base was drastically limited by the number of doors she could knock on in a day.

That's when this creative and brilliant young woman came up with her next great idea. She contacted her family, friends, and past customers—her social network—and trained them to demonstrate the ointment in customers' homes, giving prospective customers something valuable for free to make a sale. She also encouraged the women who bought and believed in her product to tell their friends—social spread—and to invite them over to their homes for coffee, tea, a demonstration of the ointment, and the chance to buy what they saw sold. Now her trained sales staff did their demonstrations not just for one woman, but for a room full of women who had gathered together with friends to see about a new product. Voilà! Social commerce!

Had Madame CJ invented social commerce? Of course not! (Remember that caveman with the chisel?) What she did invent, however, was a powerful new business model that is widely used today to sell things from makeup to kitchen products to kids' toys, and even "adult" toys. By the time she died in 1919, Madame C. J. Walker employed more than three thousand people. She left behind a prosperous business, extensive property holdings, and personal wealth in excess of $1 million. For clarity, a million dollars in 1919 is like $13.5 million today. She did this, despite the grim outlook her early life presented. She changed the way many women treated their hair, and she invented a business model that still thrives one hundred years later. Just don't blame her the next time you get invited to a social commerce party you don't want to go to! The good she did far outweighs you having to tell a friend you can't go. She brought social commerce into the twentieth century, and now I'm going to help you make the most of the twenty-first-century version.

Thanks to technology, we have advantages that Madame CJ couldn't begin to dream about. As we make our way through this book together, we're going to examine strategies and learn techniques for making today's social scene work to our business advantage. I am a businessman, first, last, and always. My goal is not unlike Madame CJ's. Sure, I want to stay creative, try intriguing new business models, and explore potentially rich sources of new customers. But above all these things, I am all about making money. Throughout the next twelve chapters, you'll hear me say, lots of times, "If what I'm doing is not earning me money, I don't have time for it. If it don't make dollars, it don't make sense."

SOCIAL. SOCIAL. SOCIAL. SOCIAL.

Throughout the past decade, most of the world has been fascinated with the technologies—first dubbed Web 2.0—now known as the social web. In all this rush to get onto the social web, you'll hear people talking about social networks as social media, social media as social marketing, and all kinds of things called social commerce. Let's get the definition straight now, so we can move into our work together with our vocabulary in place. These terms are *not* interchangeable. Not even close. All kinds of trouble will follow business owners who set out on social media thinking that all they have to do is sprinkle social networks with their products and brand, and that this alone will lead to successful social commerce. We need a clear and simple way to distinguish these terms from one another so that we can make the most of the powerful tools that lie just behind the words.

Compound Word	Minus	Real Meaning
Social Media -	*Social* =	**Media**
Social Marketing -	*Social* =	**Marketing**
Social Networking -	*Social* =	**Networking**
Social Commerce -	*Social* =	**Commerce**

Figure 1-1

7

If you simply remove the common denominator here (social), you can now get back to the roots of the terms and see that they are far from interchangeable (see Figure 1-1). They aren't even close. Media does not equal marketing, although you can use the media to market your products and services. Marketing is not networking, although you can use your network to make contacts for marketing. Of course, commerce stands in a world all by itself. For our purposes, it is and will continue to be the most important term in this book. Commerce, by definition, is all activities, functions, and institutions involved in transferring goods or services from product producers to end-user consumers. Okay, that's reasonable, and I agree.

Commerce is and always has been about products, consumers, manufacturers, and retailers. Just because you put the term "social" in front of it does not change the meaning of the word. I want to hear that cash register ring—*ka-ching*! If that's not happening, it's not commerce. Throughout this book, I'm going to show you how to use social media to build your presence on social networks so you can use social marketing to achieve real profits through social commerce. I don't care about "Likes" on Facebook. I'm not interested in how many followers you have on Twitter. And you can't post enough images on Instagram to impress me. If you aren't ringing up sales, you have not achieved social commerce success. *Period.*

♠ BREAKING **THE ICE**

The Power of Social Commerce Is in the Tools

I am happy to be the one to tell you this is 100 percent wrong! The power behind social commerce is the same today as it was in Madame CJ's day. It's the *people*, people! That is how it all began and that is how it will continue to be long after Facebook and Twitter are laughably old-fashioned. As we begin this journey together, I don't want you to forget: You are here to sell your goods and services to people. You are not here to become a big shot on any social network.

THE POWER OF SOCIAL MEDIA

Social commerce is our goal, and to achieve this goal we'll use social media tools. I think social media is an incredibly powerful thing. So powerful that I believe it saved network TV. If you look back over the last three or four years, you may remember a time when the buzz was all about how no one was watching network TV anymore. With so many media choices, poor ol' network TV didn't stand a chance. You can have a thousand cable channels. You can watch everything on Netflix and Hulu. You have social media and YouTube competing, and winning, the battle for people's spare time. Yep, the end of network TV was near. Until the people at the TV networks decided to take advantage of social media and combine it with their TV shows. It was almost the perfect merging of the old and the new.

While social media sites were taking us away from TV, broadcasters were focusing on lots of different competition shows. From singing wannabes to dancing stars, people tuned in to watch weekly competitions. Programs such as *American Idol* and *Dancing with the Stars* became huge hits. People made the time to watch the competitions unfold. A new wrinkle added to these shows was that they had to be watched live. The experience didn't work if you set your DVR. Why? Because success for the hopeful contestants was based on viewer votes. If you wanted to vote, you had to watch the live performance. If you cared enough to vote, you wanted to watch the second evening to get the results and see if your contestant was still safe. Making this even more compelling was that even if you didn't watch the live show, you couldn't help but find out the results whether you wanted to or not. Once the shows were over, the results were splashed all over Twitter and Facebook. It was that immediate.

Well, a few years into this frenzy, along came *The Voice*. No one held out too much hope for it. The market was saturated by competition shows, and amateur singers were all over the place. Ha! This new show wouldn't have the chops to compete with the giant *American Idol*. The latecomer, however, came in with some new tricks, with the most powerful one introduced in the second season. The people behind *The Voice* added social media to the mix. They created the Social Media Lounge where they could share with viewers what people had been saying on the social networks about the performances they'd just watched. The following year, they started sharing this input in real time. They pulled tweets from Twitter and pushed them out to the audience at home during the competition. That's how important audience engagement has become.

Audience engagement began to spread to other shows. Now the producers of programs like *America's Next Top Model* began taking social media into account as a voting platform. It's not just about the judges, even when it seems to be. People who produce shows want to keep viewers engaged, just like you want to keep your customers connected. If these producers can determine who is trending, whether because they're popular or obnoxiously entertaining, they know who their viewers are most connected to. The popular contestants add value to the show, but so does the drama caused by the obnoxious contestants. If it were up to you to keep your viewership high, would you send the nasty contestant who gets all the media buzz home, or would you cut the less dramatic contestant who does everything right except create publicity?

The most innovative TV social media integration I have seen is Bravo TV's *Watch What Happens Live*, with Bravo's Andy

Cohen (my man crush). He actually has real-time polls and even plays drinking games with his TV viewing audience. It's all live, interactive, and you see the results as they happen in real time.

Social media is a powerhouse of crowdsourcing, and crowd-sourcing gives you some of the most accurate and powerfully truthful data you can have. I used it to help my publisher decide which cover to use for this book. I convinced the publisher to let me post the three cover choices we came up with on my social networks, including Twitter, Facebook, and Google+. I asked which one seemed most appealing. The cover you're holding in your hand was the clear winner (see Figure 1-2).

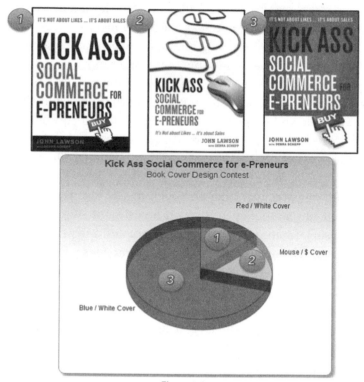

Figure 1-2

THERE'S SO MUCH TO LEARN, BUT IT'S NOT THAT HARD, FOLKS

Throughout this book, I'm going to share strategies and techniques with you for leveraging social media to achieve social commerce success. I'm not going to lie, there's a lot to learn, but I also want to assure you it is not difficult to do. I hear it from people all the time. Business owners tell me they've spent hours creating campaigns and content. Some of them have spent real money hiring "experts" to help them get their businesses on social media. After spending all this time and even money, they may find they have "Likes" or "followers." But what they don't have is increased sales, and they're not making more money. That may be social media success, but that's not the same as success in social commerce. I can't hear the *ka-ching*.

I've been in business long enough to learn not to spend my money on things that don't bring me a solid return on my investment. And as for time? Well, that's even more valuable to me than money. I can always find ways to earn money, but time is irreplaceable and none of us knows when it will run out! I am not here to make you a "social media marketing expert." Instead, I am here to help you use these social media tools effectively to help you make more money. It's as simple as that. If we're going to spend our precious time on social media, we need to make it pay off in real money, return on investment. We're going to explore social commerce concepts, principles, and practices that are eternal. The techniques, tools, and strategies you learn here will apply no matter what new and exciting tools lay ahead. I can tell you, for sure, that those new things *are* coming.

I recently attended the South by Southwest (SXSW) conference in Austin, Texas, the largest interactive conference in the United States. I was onstage with the Original Kings of Technology (fb.com/OriginalKingsofTechnology) for a great panel discussion. While I was there, I saw the future of social technology. Sure, right now, as I write, Facebook is the number one social network. But I've seen technology splash on the scene, create wild and crazy hype, and then age out to be replaced by newer things. Can we all say "America Online"? "MySpace"? I know that today's Facebook will be replaced by the next great King of the Hill. For our purposes, it doesn't matter at all. By the end of this book, you'll be prepared for whatever comes along as we make our own marks in the eternal cyberspace we call social commerce. Who knows, maybe the next great Madame C. J. Walker is reading this book right now. So, let's get to work!

CHAPTER 2

King Consumer
Time—Find Your Match

"You will love brands when they love you first."

—Gary Vaynerchuk

S ocial media has changed a lot of what we do in life, but maybe nowhere else has this change been as apparent as in business. Consumers today don't shop the way they used to, before they had access to the opinions of billions of other people. They are far more dependent on their own social networks for advice and recommendations. In realms that change as quickly as social media and online commerce, it's easy to assume your consumer is a whole different animal, and a powerfully equipped one at that. Or is he?

I don't think the role of the customer or the consumer or the vendor has actually changed at all. Vendors and consumers and customers are eternal. There's always been a place for these different characters in the world, and they've always interacted for money. So, in that sense, as always, the consumer is king. But the consumer reigns only in a very specific sense of the word. They are the ruler of the one thing we want: what's inside his wallet. The consumers' ability to spend makes them king, lord, master, ruler, judge, and jury of all things that have to do with their outward spending.

⬆ BREAKING **THE ICE**

The Customer Is Always Right

That's ridiculous! No way. Impossible. The customer is *not* always right. But, the customer *is* always the customer and, as we've seen, the way customers control their wallets matters to your success. This supersedes all right and wrong, just as a king does. Whether or not you think the customer is right, you still have to continue to court King Consumers. They don't have to be right—they're kings.

THE KING CONSUMER?

So, everyone says the consumer is king, but now you know that's true only in one sense. The King controls the purse strings. We've also all heard that in the world of online marketing, content is king. Not true, either, content is not king. Content is the King's queenie boyfriend. He's still important, but no longer does he stand all alone as the ruler of a transaction. So if we rule out the consumer as king and we acknowledge that content is the queenie boyfriend, who *is* the King? Context is the King. If you put your content, your information, into the right context and put it in front of the right people at the right time, it transfers into commerce. They will buy.

So, with the combined power of knowing what content your consumers need and an understanding of how you place that content into the right context, you'll be ready to see some real improvement in your sales. The content of what you say hasn't changed. You still want to give your potential consumer the information necessary to make the decision to buy from you. The context dictates the manner in which you share that content, and the contact you are now able to have with your customer is the biggest and coolest thing we have going on right now.

Context + Contact = Relationship

Because we now have such powerful tools for reaching our consumers, we can begin to create a relationship with them that hasn't been possible since the days of the neighborhood stores. In those days, your favorite baker may have baked your favorite pies on Monday, knowing you'd stop by to pick one up. On a particular Monday, something may have come up to keep you from stopping by the bakery. So, when you went on Tuesday to buy the bread you needed, you'd find that your baker had saved a pie for you. He knew, even if you didn't stop by on Monday, you'd still want that pie. This kind of personal service is the result of years of transactions between vendor and customer. This type of relationship hasn't been possible with e-commerce until the growth of social media. Now, we can try to develop relationships with the consumers of our products in ways that have been impossible until fairly recently.

As you saw in Chapter 1, since the web's origins, it has been used primarily as a very social tool. The whole "you've got mail" thing was social, but the content on the web was static. The rapid way the web grew with its static content was incredible, especially with fewer people creating this content. What's different now is social media, and its users are growing exponentially. Some of the web's content is still static and some of it is old, but the majority of the content today is organic and in flux. We're watching data change in real time.

Before the growth of social media, the only way to reach your consumers was through television, radio, or print, with messages somewhat directed toward the presumed King Consumers who bought your products. The messages may have pulled the heartstrings, nudging them a little toward making a purchase, but it was a scattershot approach to promoting products.

Think about the way we get commercials. Here we have two parents and a couple of kids hanging out in the family room together to watch TV. When the laundry detergent commercial comes on, it talks about how effectively it cleans our clothes, how good they smell, how much value the detergent offers. The dad may pitch in and toss a couple loads per week into the machines. The kids may be old enough to do their own wash, but the advertisers know it is most likely to be Mom who does the shopping, and she selects the laundry detergent for the family. That product and its marketing efforts are most likely directed toward Mom, and there is no way to make it any more personal than that. She may, at some point, switch from liquid to individual little pods of detergent to help encourage her family to be more independent with the chore, but she's still the one most likely to make the decision.

Now, thanks to social media, vendors can get the content and the context of how consumers feel about a product or solution they need, and that's our goal. You want to get *their* content, *their* context, so you can create a message that better resonates with that King Consumer. Once you make that contact, that connection, you've suddenly changed the dynamics. You are no longer just trying to sell something to someone. You are now having a conversation with your customer. You are now actually in the mix—a part of the equation. You are part of the conversation your customers are having about an issue or need or desire. Now you can prepare to fulfill those needs for them.

Being a part of the conversation allows you to get closer to your customers than ever before. Now, we're no longer trying to throw stuff out there, spray it, and pray that it works. You don't need to spend your time and money that way anymore because, since you've joined the conversation, you have a much clearer idea of what King Consumers really want. They've given you the keys to the kingdom! Now you can use their language and their issues to make a real connection with them, not the generic kind of connection that was the only one TV or radio or print allowed you to make. Now you've made a simple, genuine connection with all their needs, which you can fulfill. And all of those other things your King Consumers are talking about, well, you won't even pay attention to those. What matters most is that you can really lock it down and deal with the needs you can fulfill, enabling you to create messaging that is both very specific and very effective.

🔥 BREAKING **THE ICE**

The Modern King Consumer: Empowered

Everyone wants to talk about how "empowered" the modern consumer is. It annoys me. They're no more empowered than they ever were. They're really not. The only thing they are empowered with is a bigger voice, because of the technology. But you, the seller, have that same empowerment. You use the same tools they do.

Okay, I guess it's easier for a person to post a bad review on a blog or a page than it once was to walk up and down the street with a sandwich sign reading, "I hate this company," like the guy in Figure 2-1, but it's essentially the same thing.

Figure 2-1

People used to walk past the guy carrying that sign to shop at that store anyway, and people today will still go past a negative comment about you, too. The people who make these kinds of statements are turning away only a small number of other people, if any at all, and so these actions affect a very small percentage of sales for a corporation. That is, unless it's something really big and it gets pushed out there and goes viral.

In 2009 a video protest against United Airlines went viral. It seems a hapless musician, traveling with his band, watched as United Airlines baggage handlers threw his guitar case around on the tarmac, resulting in irreparable damage to the instrument. Dissatisfied with the lack of response from United, he and his friends created a video named "United Breaks Guitars" and posted it to YouTube. Now it has more than 12 million views (and probably many more by the time you read this). Clearly, United should have just replaced the guitar in the first place and moved on!

But we can count on one hand how many people have actually affected a large company with a campaign that gets picked up and goes viral. Anything *can* go viral, but that's always the exception, not the rule. That's why we call it a virus. If it were the rule it wouldn't be viral, because then everything would be viral and, consequently, we'd have to up the ante to make something viral. So don't be intimidated by the newly "empowered" King Consumers. They're not that powerful, unless they can write a good country song, in which case, fix it fast.

HOW DOES THE KING SHOP?

Although it's clear that the nature of the King Consumer hasn't essentially changed, the manner by which consumers go about shopping certainly has. For most of the history of this relationship between vendor and consumer, information has been the key to making purchasing decisions. Internet shopping has made gathering that information easier and quicker, but we're still talking about static information. Your job as a vendor has always been to provide robust content that tells your customers all about the benefits of your products. That's why content has long held such a vital place in the world of online commerce.

Even with the most robust and well-planned content you can provide, Internet shopping has long had certain disadvantages that keep the King Consumer relatively skeptical. There are trust issues. At first, it seemed complicated. Nothing has been able to completely eliminate the consumers' need to touch and feel the product, experiencing it as completely as is possible outside the virtual marketplace. Until the growth of social media, all we could gain from Internet shopping was information. Experience was simply not an option.

Social media now gives us all the experience of shopping, and that has made a difference in the way online consumers shop. If you want to know the experience of buying, owning, or using a product, the information is still easy to find. That's the label, and it contains all the content the online vendor shares to make the King want to select a particular item. But social media goes way beyond that label. If a consumer wants to open the package, lift off the top, and see what's inside the bottle, she is able to do that through social media. When you can get to that level of understanding, a whole different world opens up.

Now consumers can ask questions within their own social spheres. When they ask a question on social media, they don't just get the static information available on the label, but something more. Social media gives perspectives about the organic experiences of the people who answer questions there. We're no longer getting just the facts. We're also sharing in the experience by getting opinions and informed advice. Do your customers' organic experiences with your products or services represent information that is more accurate or true than the information you were previously getting from a conscientious vendor? Of course not, but you can already get all that information and more with just a few keystrokes. As a business owner, the answers you receive on social media are information that has been filtered through the process of experience, which makes it a whole different platform. Consumers think about your responses in a completely different way. And that's why you have to talk to your consumers completely differently as well. The consumer who grew up looking for information is not the same consumer we have now in an environment of experience.

♠ BREAKING **THE ICE**

Your Consumer Is Unique

M irror, mirror on the web ... This updated snippet of the old fairy tale rhyme illustrates that, even today, people still compare themselves to everyone else. No one is unique. It doesn't matter how "out there" she wants to think she is, she's not. No one stands alone. Humans are innately designed to mirror the actions and behaviors of other humans. We've always done it, and we always will.

Of course this is the way babies learn to relate to others. Have you ever watched an adult spoon-feed a baby? The adult opens her mouth with each bite she offers to the child. She even makes chewing motions, even though she's not the one eating! And it doesn't stop as we grow up.

Let's take a look at the growth of tattoos among young adults. Most of these adults didn't start dreaming of tattoos soon after they left their high chairs. Most of them didn't spend their childhoods planning and dreaming of the ink they were going to spread all up and down their bodies. But, at some point in their youth, someone they thought was pretty cool decided to add some ink. Now part of the reason why that person was cool was simply the fact the he'd gotten a tattoo. In typical humanlike behavior, his social cohorts wanted to think of themselves as being just as cool as he was. They may not have been able to replicate his coolness in many other ways, but they *could* get inked. They saw themselves through the "mirror" of his tattoo and decided they wanted to have the same reflection. Many don't even realize when they're mirroring.

This mirroring happens all the time as people choose products. In sales trainings, new salespeople are taught how to mirror their customers, especially when it comes time to close the deal. You may have heard that when you're ready to nail down the price, lean back to appear more open and friendly. If you lean forward, you appear overanxious and even a bit threatening. It happens online, too, as people share opinions about their choices. You can take full advantage of that subconscious, innate human trait and provide the mirror you know your consumer wants to find her reflection in.

Opinion Versus Fact

Today's online consumer is looking for opinions instead of facts. The facts are just so easy to get, they don't even need to worry about how they're going to find them. There's so much information available now that it's actually harder *not* to find out the details of a particular product than it is to find them. People online are using social media to gather opinions, and the crazy thing about this is that people will default to opinions even when they are disproved by facts! Is opinion greater than fact? I don't know. Let's look at a long-standing disagreement among online sellers, free shipping versus paid shipping.

Clearly, many online sellers are reluctant to offer free shipping. From their perspective it will increase their overall costs and diminish their profits. The opinion is that free shipping doesn't work. The actual data shows that free shipping does increase sales, but some online sellers will listen still to those idiots talking about not offering free shipping. Show them the facts, and that still won't change their opinion that free shipping doesn't work.

King Consumers also operate within this realm where opinion matters more than fact, and they've been trained to take the opinions they hear to heart. Since your consumers now operate within the realm of opinion, you, the merchant, will have to offer more opinion and less fact. This gives you a tremendous opportunity to place yourself in the role of opinion leader. Your job now is to research and learn the opinions consumers are sharing.

⬇ ICE MAKER

Educate Yourself About Your Consumers' Conversations

Your job, and you need to begin right now, is to search social media conversations for products you sell. Start grasping the tone and language and any other details. You'll need to understand your consumers' jargon as well as any recurring issues and past disappointments they may have had. The more aware you become of the world these consumers inhabit and what they've experienced, the more effectively you'll be able to reach them by speaking their own language. Social media has changed the consumer and the shopping experience, and it's vitally important that you learn how.

The Kings Are Finding, Not Searching

The most natural outcome of this switch from data to opinion is that your consumers are more likely to find their purchases rather than search for them. Rather than spend time online researching the facts about which item will best suit their needs, they directly ask their social networks about it instead. For example, "Which phone should I buy?" is posted on a few networks and within hours, if not minutes, this shopper will have recommendations from people she has already vetted and included in her social sphere. Once enough friends have responded with their recommendations, including the reasons why one phone is preferred over another one, our shopper will have a small list of potential phones and her research can now begin. As you can see in Figure 2-2, it's quick and easy.

Figure 2-2

Consumers used to start their buying decisions by researching features, materials, construction, and warranties. Now they're just asking their friends. A friend responds with, "I just bought phone XYZ." Your consumer is now a lot more likely to click through and take a look at this recommended item, but this is not searching. It's more like finding. Your consumer began just by wondering about which phone she might want, but then she was influenced to "want" the one her trusted friend likes. Our consumer didn't set out to research all possible phones, only to begin a conversation. As online influence becomes more the norm for shopping online, social networks will adapt to reflect this. Pinterest is the perfect example. Pinterest is the composite of what people "find" as they wander around online. Consumers do not search for a particular thing so they can build a Pinterest board. They organically create these collections of images as they find things that appeal to them.

The King Is Mobile

It's impossible to miss the impact that mobile devices have had on the world in this part of the twenty-first century. Spend an hour waiting at the gate in any airport in the United States, and you'll see mostly the tops of the heads of your fellow travelers. No one is watching the action on the tarmac as planes come and go, and people-watching has fallen off as a pastime. Nearly all travelers are focused on the devices in the palms of their hands. Wherever humans decide to spend time, they ultimately end up making purchases, and your King Consumer is no different. This device is filled with ads and their phones are full of purchased content like games, apps, music, movies, etc.

According to comScore, the leader in analytic measuring of all things digital, mobile commerce is on the upswing. In a report published in September 2012, the company stated that four out of every five smartphone users, a whopping 85.9 million of us in the third quarter of that year, visited retail sites with their mobile devices. As you might guess, the giant in mobile commerce is currently Amazon, with reportedly 49.6 million unique visitors in the same period. eBay also scored 32.6 million visitors to its website. Many of these same shoppers are just waiting for you to court them, too. Using comScore's data, you can see more clearly who among your potential consumers will most likely be placing orders through their phones.

- Seventy percent of phone shoppers are under the age of forty-five.
- Women shoppers spend more than men do on mobile.
- Women spend more time on retail sites then men do.
- Unique views on mobile are about 50/50 based on gender.

Mobile commerce offers you the opportunity to cash in on impulse shopping. With a device always in hand, your consumers can see someone using a product, decide they like the mirror image that person reflects, and, within seconds, have one of their very own on its way to their own homes. Tapjoy.com, a mobile advertising and mobilization platform, reported to the website

BizReport in October 2012 that by 2015 mobile commerce will have expanded by 300 percent! Reported by the website Daily Deal Media in November 2012, some parts of the world, including the United Kingdom, have already begun to see this dramatic growth. So, as you consider who your King Consumer might be, don't forget that it's almost a guarantee he or she will be a mobile shopper.

WHO IS *YOUR* KING CONSUMER?

Now that you understand how social media has changed the nature and behavior of the King Consumer, it's time to turn your focus more directly to the consumers who represent your own particular royalty. No matter what you're selling, there is a particular person who will shop for and buy your products. It's a very universal principle, but each vendor has to figure out who that is for him- or herself.

I hear it all the time. Businesspeople will say, "We sell to everybody and anybody." I'd love to sell to everybody, but I don't want to sell to just anyone. I want a particular person to buy from me, a person who wants to buy the products I sell. What you're going to do now is create your ideal business scenario and populate it with the type of person you know will want your product. To do this, you have to use a bit of imagination, and it's here that you can have some fun. Use technology to help you find the fun, or crayons or markers—whatever tools will let your imagination roam. When you're all finished, you'll have a specific customer in mind. Next, you'll create your content in a way that lets you speak specifically to this manufactured customer in the language he or she will respond to. Now you can include that language in your social media, e-mails, and keyword searches. Repeat this exercise so that you have one sample customer for each gender.

❄ ICE MAKER

Your Very Own King Consumer

Give each of your manufactured customers a name. It doesn't matter—David, Mary, Aisha—as long as your consumers have a specific persona. Now let's get to the questions you'll ask about this person, and the answers you'll use to better address your King Consumer. Get as detailed and specific as you can with your answers:

- What is the predominant gender of your consumers?
- Are they married? Do they have children?
- What kind of work does Mary do?
- How much money does Aisha make?
- How old is David?
- What kind of car does Mary drive?
- How much time do they spend online and where do they spend it?
- What is the size of their usual orders?
- How often does she buy?
- Does he run out of this item? If so, how often?
- Does David shop on impulse?
- Does Mary buy based on need or want?

At the end of this experiment, you'll have a single person who represents a conglomerate of your average customer, both male and female. Over time, you will refine this profile as you learn more about your consumers and their shopping habits. But once you complete this exercise, you'll be speaking to one specific person.

SUMO LESSON

When I started to sell doo rags, my assumption was to add this item to my inventory of urban accessories. I figured the city kids would want to buy from me, and so I proceeded with that assumption. It wasn't long before I came to see that I was very wrong about this. Most of my customers were coming, not from urban centers on the East or West Coast, but from rural places in the Midwest. My customers were largely white farm kids! They didn't use doo rags for the same purposes that urban guys did.

An African-American teen will comb his hair out as straight as possible and put a doo rag on to create waves instead of curls. Of course, he can go around the corner to the local store and find an abundant supply of doo rags in his own neighborhood. He views it as a tool as much as a fashion statement. The white kid in Oklahoma loves hip-hop and rap and wants to wear a doo rag to feel cool. He wants to mirror the culture that he thinks makes him cool. I was using the language of the urban kids, and the rural kids were still buying. I also learned a lot of cyclists wear doo rags under their helmets.

By studying the analytics of who my customers really were, I gained insights into how to craft different product descriptions for the different types of customers I was actually serving, not the customers I thought I'd be serving. Now I have three different approaches for selling the same product, and my messages effectively target the three different categories of my King Consumer.

That's a Rap!

✔ I understand that the consumer is King in only a very limited sense of the word.
✔ The combination of content in the right context presented at the right time will result in commerce.
✔ Social commerce has empowered the seller as much as the consumer.
✔ Today's consumer shops differently from the way consumers shopped before social commerce.
✔ I can educate myself about my King Consumers' tastes and opinions.
✔ My potential customers are most often being drawn to products, not searching for them.
✔ I have clear ideas about who is likely to buy from me.

CHAPTER 3

Me Commerce—
It's All About Me, Bro

"Float like a butterfly, sting like a bee."

—*Muhammad Ali*

N ow you have a clear mental image of your King Consumer. If you completed the exercise from Chapter 2,
you know a lot about the people who may actually want to buy the
products you sell. Getting as specific as you can has allowed you
to keep these individuals in the back of your mind as you move
your social commerce plans forward. Now let's take a look at the
world your King Consumer occupies online, which has changed
dramatically in the years since we all started shopping on the
Internet. It is important for you to understand those changes
if you are going to successfully reach your target consumers
and turn them into customers. First let's define the term "Me
Commerce."

Me Commerce is a term I've coined for the concept of millennial commerce. So what? Millennial commerce is the difference
between where we were at the beginning of this journey through
commerce—e-commerce—all the way until now. It's being able
to move beyond just the electronic part and back toward a more
social interaction. Me Commerce is constantly running on top
of the online social sphere, because the lines between gathering

online and shopping have blurred significantly. A decade ago, people went online to shop. They had their favorite destinations, and transactions were conducted mostly between vendor and customer. There wasn't nearly as much consumer-to-consumer socializing going on. Today that is all different.

Now people are getting together online in ways they were never able to gather before, and as they converge, they're making transactions. It's a more organic approach to online shopping. Living online through social media is very personalized, and that's what Me Commerce is all about. We have an entire generation now that has grown up with social media as their primary platform for communication, and they will be the best minds and wage earners in our country for the foreseeable future. Young people today have grown up online with both e-commerce and social media. That fact is changing the way we reach these customers and the way we conduct business transactions in this millennial commerce environment.

LET'S TAKE A LOOK BACK TO THE FUTURE

You may have heard from many that when it comes to web-marketing success, "content is king." In an e-commerce world where content was king, making your listings and product descriptions stand out with exact and complete information was the way to distinguish yourself from your competitors. Throw in great images and you were pretty much exactly where you wanted to be. But, as you know now, that was before people stopped searching and making purchasing decisions based strictly on facts. Now you're going to have to find a better way to stand out from other online vendors. You still need to make a case for your customers needing or wanting your products, but now you'll make that case and present it to your customers in their own environments and in their own way of speaking.

↟ BREAKING THE ICE

Social Commerce? Nah, Social Spam, Instead

How many times have you heard this same old advice? "Find where people are talking. Join the conversation and bring them to your website." I hate it every time I hear it. That's all about what you should do, but it doesn't help you if you don't know how you should do it. People who recommend this are looking at the old e-commerce model of putting the details out there and getting a sale in return. It doesn't work that way anymore. Experts will tell you to just go on Facebook and search for Levi jeans. You'll find people mentioning the brand, you'll see where they are hanging out, and then you can start spamming the hell out of them. Sites like eBay and Amazon will put social buttons on pages, and then the third-party sellers will go and press those buttons. Have you been told to post all your items in tweets on Twitter, because that's a good social strategy? Oh, come on—really? This is all just social spam, and we already get way too much of that crap. Plus, in today's world of Me Commerce, your customers are far too sophisticated not to see right through it. You may enter a crowded room at a party and yell out, "I sell blue widgets!" You may even sell a widget this way, but 99.98 percent of your fellow partygoers will still think you're a jackass. That's not how you want to appear to your King Consumers.

There's got to be a better way to begin the conversation. There is and, lucky for you, I'm about to tell you how. But first, you'll need to forget a lot of what you've been told is true. Social commerce requires that your marketing efforts be different from what they were even five years ago. We've left the world of "push marketing" behind us, and there's no going back. Push marketing is when you use various marketing channels to get your message in front of your ideal client. The marketer is in control of what the message is, how it is seen, and when and where it appears. Pushing content out to your customers may still work on TV, and it may have once been a successful strategy for you, too, but not anymore.

Now You're on a Two-Way Street

Social commerce is a *dialogue* between vendor and consumer. The key here is that first syllable, "di," as in two. We humans are physiologically formed with faces, which should give us a hint about how to proceed with a non-spam campaign in social commerce. If you've noticed, we have two ears, two eyes, two nostrils, and only one mouth. This suggests that we should be gathering information in quantities twice as large as the information we're spouting out. If you're searching for your customers on social media so that you can talk to them, you're already missing the most important part of social commerce. You should be searching for your customers, first of all, to listen to them. When you find your King Consumers on social media, the very first thing you want to do is observe them.

Standard old marketing was all about the monologue. A clear definition of marketing is "the process of communicating the value of a product or service to your customer." Of course you still want to communicate the value of your products to your consumers, but you're going to have to reassess the old standard Five P's of Marketing: product, price, promotion, place, and people. These P's translated into knowing your product, setting your price, creating your promotion and locating it in the place your customers turned to for information, and understanding who those customers were.

The Five P's of Social Commerce today are platform, perspective, participate, personal, and pure. Each social network is a separate and distinct platform. You won't use the same language or expressions on LinkedIn that you will on Twitter, of course, but you also won't approach Facebook the same way you use LinkedIn. It's important for you to distinguish the platforms from one another, because your consumers do. You have to understand your consumers' perspectives and what they use their social networks for. You have to understand the mind-set they bring to each platform—it's different! Your messages have to be personal and at the same time, pure. We've all been so overloaded by spam online that unless your message has a personal approach and a level of purity, you won't be any different from that blue-widget guy at the party. Finally, you'll participate with your consumers, but not until you clearly understand the contextual relevancy, and you've honed your content to go along with that.

When you've successfully engaged the Five P's of Social Commerce, you're ready to rework your blog content, your sales copy, and your website to ensure that your online persona is as personal and pure as you can make it.

⬇ ICE MAKER

How Do You Find Your Consumers' Conversations?

Why not try asking your current customers about this? Do a survey and ask them three to five questions about how they use social media, or if they use it at all. Ask them to "friend" you on Facebook. Tell them you'll follow them on Twitter if they let you know their Twitter handle (and in all likelihood, of course, they in turn will follow you). These actions can help you find the niche areas on the web where your customers reside. Then once you get there, what will you do? You will listen and observe.

Once we find our consumers in conversation, what exactly are we listening for? We're confirming those five old W's of journalism we used as you created the persona of your King Consumer: who, what, where, when, and why. Let's go a little deeper with those now.

Who is talking? Is it someone who is already a customer? Is it someone just gathering information about the products? Is this person joining in on the conversation without any interest in buying the item, just wanting to share opinions about it?

What are they talking about? Where are they talking about it? When are they talking about it? Was it before an online shopping transaction occurred or after

Finally, we'll ask why they are talking about it. We're looking for the sentiment here. Is it positive or negative about your brand or product?

Me Commerce Is Largely About Vanity

Living life on social networks allows each of us to feed our own vanity. The whole system is built with the understanding that humans are vain. Why would we think our online networks care about the minutiae of our daily lives if it weren't for vanity? We can make an announcement on Facebook, telling our online cohorts that we've participated in a charity, for example, and we can expect many "Likes" in return. It feeds something within each of us to believe so many people actually care about how we spent our Saturday morning this week. From the very beginning, when humans first started gathering on those dinosaurs we called "online services," vanity played a key role.

Behind the keyboard you can be whoever it is you want to be. If you think you're too short, you can make yourself appear taller. If you think you're too large, you can trim the pictures to appear slimmer. Too old? Not anymore! At the time of this writing, this phenomenon is being played out on a very popular MTV show, *Catfish*. This show, based on a movie of the same name, takes an online relationship and moves it into physical reality. The two twenty-something male hosts lead the weekly adventure by choosing an individual, and then work to unite that person with the online lover he or she has been pursuing. It's a fascinating study in vanity.

Not only does the object of the lovelorn get to be whoever he or she claims to be, but the poor lovesick sucker actually believes it. In some instances, these two "lovers" have been communicating for years. The party wishing to take the relationship to the next step is so eager for this love to be everything he's come to believe it is, that he's willing to deny all reality and accept that for the past two or three years, his lover has been "too busy" to meet him in person. Something always seems to come up every time they plan a get-together—even if they live only fifteen minutes apart! What makes an adult, even a young one, so willing to suspend all logic and disbelief? The main reason is vanity.

Usually the reluctant parties have posted pictures of themselves online that are hugely desirable, according to our current standards. The people who fall for this are so eager to feed their own vanity—their belief that they are attractive and desirable enough to warrant this attention from someone so hot—that although something may not smell right, they are still willing to take the next step and commit to the face-to-face meeting. The reluctant partners, in every single case so far, were clearly not who they claimed to be, but the lovelorn still pursued the relationships in the vague hope that their good sense will be proven wrong.

This is so important for you to understand, because you are an individual, too. We all have some of these different ways of expressing ourselves on social media that we wish we could use in the real world. We can be far bigger on social networks than we could be otherwise, and this is a real boon to you as you express your passion for your products and what they can do for your customers. While discussing your products, you can offer to friend your customers on Facebook and follow them on Twitter, which feeds their vanity and desire to belong to a larger group, and it helps you share information about your products, too; as long as you're doing it with purity and in a personal manner. It's vanity that allows you to tailor your messages, content, and communications to a variety of your consumers and do it in a genuine and appealing way.

Everything Old Is New Again

That old saying, "There's nothing new under the sun," doesn't take social commerce into account. You've already seen this *is* a new means and opportunity to relate to your consumers in new and exciting ways. You have new tools for gaining insights, vocabulary, entry, and access to your consumers that you didn't have just a few years ago. But that doesn't mean you have to invent whole new ways to relate to your consumers. You just have to learn how to apply some of the old sales and marketing techniques to this newer genre of sales. Let's compare the old door-to-door vacuum salesman to the new world of Me Commerce. Knocking on individual doors is not something anyone wants to do in 2014, but the theory behind this technique is still a valid one. You need only to relate these principles to the new world of social commerce.

Step One: Knock on the door. This is joining the network and creating your profile. We're preparing ourselves to engage in what's going on. Here's where the home owner, in this case Mom, opens the door to see who is on the porch. The salesman there has on his best and most sincere face. Your online profile will do the same.

Step Two: Greet your customer. The salesman might tip his hat and say good morning but, in your case, you'll just say hello: "Hi, I'm here. I'm John." Mom would respond with a greeting and so will many of the people occupying the platform you've just joined. They will welcome you, because that's what people in social networks do.

Step Three: Engage in a brief conversation. The salesman might compliment the porch flowers or notice the kids' sports equipment in the yard. Mom might offer a cup of coffee. With a little conversation, the two may find out that their kids go to the same school or play on the same teams. You'll engage your consumers in similar small talk. You're prepping them for a sales pitch, but you're not yet selling anything.

Step Four: Demo your product and give something away. The salesman might notice the hallway or even the living room could use a vacuuming. He will offer Mom a little break by doing that small chore for her with his wonderful new vacuum. He doesn't ask for anything in return yet; it's a freebie. You will do the same thing. You'll offer your new friends a report you prepared or a nice coupon. Once you've given something away, people innately feel the need to return the favor.

Step Five: Close the deal. This is the call to action. For the vacuum salesman this is where he'd explain the easy payment plan and the bonus tool kit if the sale is sealed today. For you it could be "click this link," "sign up for this list," or whatever you might want these consumers to do. Just remember, this is the last step, and it has to happen only after you've carefully completed all the other steps. This way, your call to action comes from a member, in good standing, of the community you've joined. Since you're already a contributor to the community, your sales call comes across more as a way for you to solve a problem and less as a way to earn some money.

MAKING YOUR CASE IN A ME COMMERCE WORLD

Now the vacuum salesman in our previous example didn't knock on the door to make friends with the housewife. He knocked on her door to sell her a vacuum. You may care about the issues your consumers are discussing about your products, but you're not joining social networks to make new friends across cyberspace. Friendship may not matter to you any more than it mattered to the guy carrying the vacuum door to door. You can take all this Me Commerce vanity, all you've learned about transforming your consumers into customers, and use it to your best advantage. Using the Five P's of Social Commerce, you can identify the *platform* your customers use. Through careful observation you can gain insight into the *perspectives* they share about many things, including your products and the needs they fulfill. You can then *participate* in the conversation, making that participation *personal* and *pure*. You can make sure that your content is strong in the context where your consumers reside, and that will result in transactions.

So, in a world occupied by people telling only partial truths about who they are and what they're doing, why do you need to be personal and pure? Because you're joining these social spaces with the intent to sell, not befriend. You can use the vanity of social media to sell, but you have to do it in a way that seems genuine to avoid the online spamming that everyone hates. I want my brand to represent a persona in social commerce, and I'm going to use the media to create however many personas I'm going to need to sell my products. I want the people I interact with online to envision the lifestyle my products and services will bring to their lives, and I'm going to create my content to support and represent that lifestyle.

Consider the Progressive insurance lady, Flo. She doesn't really sell Progressive insurance. She doesn't really offer advice for insurance consumers. Insider tip: She probably doesn't care that much about your insurance troubles and it's not like she really answers the phone! Flo is the face of her company. She's a person who people can relate to, and so is that Gecko from GEICO. They both participate in the conversation about insurance. They're both perfectly well suited to their platforms.

They're both personal, and they're both pure. It's much easier to believe that Flo cares about your insurance needs than it is to believe a faceless insurance company does. And so, every time that Progressive wants to sell you insurance, they bring out dear, sweet Flo.

As you create your personas online, you have the same freedom to be whoever you wish to be. You can create multiple personas, depending on the different ways people use your products, and actually you should. If you have employees handling your social commerce efforts, let them be real pure people online. Let them create their personas so that the information they put out in your name will still be personal and pure. Let's look at how this might work with a specific product. Consider the folding chair.

People buy folding chairs for many different reasons, such as for attending sporting events and outdoor concerts, and for picnicking, going to the beach, and about a million other things. The person who buys a folding chair to go to her child's soccer games may be different from the person who is going to a picnic, and that person may be different from the beachgoer or concert attendee. This gives you the tremendous opportunity to engage each type of your King Consumer with targeted and specific copy that speaks personally and purely to their needs. At the outset, you'll have to create and tweak your messages for each group, but the more groups you can target with the right content in the right context, the more folding chairs you'll sell, and the more you'll seem to be a trusted persona who can solve the problems of the people on the social networks where you now reside with your customers. In this way, you'll bring your products to life and lay them at the feet of people who are likely to want them. Potential customers may not even realize what you've done, but it doesn't matter. They'll still be willing to give you money for the product your persona represents.

❆ ICE MAKER

If You Want Answers, Ask Some Questions

Now that you have some very clear ideas about who your King Consumers are and where they reside, it's time to do some fact-checking with your actual customers. I've learned a lot about what I didn't know about my customers by simply asking them. To get this information, you'll set up a quick and easy questionnaire that you can send to your customers. There are two kinds of people in this world: ones who will fill out a short questionnaire and ones who will not. You can count on a 3 to 7 percent response rate, and that is about all you need for a sampling.

Ask your customers the following questions:

1. How was your service with us?
2. What did you like best about the transaction?
3. Are there any areas that need improvement?
4. Do you use social media?
5. Would you please follow us on Twitter and Like our Face-book page? In turn we will do the same! (Include your social buttons and links but be sure to *ask* them verbally. The key is that you have not 'cause you ask not. You're asking what is important.)

You do *not* have to ask the exact same questions as above, but you get the general idea. Here's what these questions will provide. The first three questions are about the transaction. I like to get the general feedback, we all do, *but even more important*, we are asking for comments, both positive and negative. This gives your customers an opportunity to provide valuable feedback, and it offers unsatisfied customers a place to vent and be heard. Better here than on social media, right?

The last two questions are about using social commerce, and the answers will give you a feel for how many of them do. In answering question four, they may also tell you where they hang out online and why.

It's the final question that is the *gold* mine. All the other questions were just a lead-in to question five. This question asks your customers to take an action. You're asking them to follow you on social media. In this example I said I would follow them back. That's for the audience concerned with how many followers they have—vanity. You can offer anything you want here—a 10 percent coupon, a chance to win a free iPad. I don't care what it is, but make sure to offer them something for taking action. The better your offer, the better responses you will get. This information will be invaluable as we move into the next chapter and begin to work the magic that will steal your King Consumers' hearts and keep them safely in your grasp.

SUMO LESSON

And now it's time for a quiz.

I was relaxing by the pool in my backyard when I noticed the grass needed to be mowed, because there were all these little white flowers that appear when the grass gets too high. My yard looked like an open field. Dozens, maybe hundreds, of bumblebees were scurrying about from flower to flower. I thought to myself, What is it these bees are doing? I have flown around the world and spoken at dozens of conferences in dozens of countries, and I've asked this same question to every audience, so I'll ask you: What were these bees doing?

If you're like my audiences you're eager to jump in with the answer. They're pollinating. Every single time I get that answer and every single time that answer is wrong. Maybe once, someone had the right answer, but his voice was drowned out by everyone else, in the crowd, calling out "pollinating." The bee is not consciously pollinating. The flower is pollinating. The bee is collecting nectar so it can go back to the hive and make honey. The flower has evolved in such a way as to get the bee to do the pollinating! It just sits there and lets the bees do all the work (see Figure 3-1).

Figure 3-1

What nectar do you need to create to attract your "bees" so they will then collect your message and deposit it to the next place they visit online? Apple makes its customers feel cool. Owning its products therefore makes me cool. The cool factor is Apple's nectar. You are so enthralled by the coolness, you're willing to pay way more simply to have the Apple brand product. Use this lesson to begin to optimize your message for human consumption. Write *not* for the Google bots that will pick up your keywords, but for the human bee who will take your message and fly all over the web with it.

That's a Rap!

✔ I know the difference between e-commerce and Me Commerce.

✔ Successful social commerce is not as simple as finding your Consumer Kings and spamming them with ads.

✔ When I locate my King Consumers, I will observe twice as much as I contribute.

✔ I can use some of the old marketing techniques, but I need to understand how to use them in the new context of the Five P's of Social Commerce.

✔ I understand the role of vanity in the Me Commerce world, and I can use it to my best advantage.

✔ I understand that when communicating with my King Consumers, I have to present a personal and pure persona, and I know why.

CHAPTER 4

The **Five-Finger Discount**: Steal the Heart of the King Consumer

"A dream doesn't become reality through magic; it takes sweat, determination, and hard work."

—Colin Powell

Okay folks, so after reading the last two chapters you should now understand who your King Consumers are and the environment in which those kings are shopping. Now we're going to turn our attention to a plan that will help you snag King Consumers, make them fall in love with your products and services, and come back time and again to buy more. Sounds almost too good to be true? It's really not.

When I was a boy my friends and I spent mostly every Saturday at the movie matinees in Times Square. For very little money we'd watch every kung fu movie that played. My favorite one of all time was *The 5 Fingers of Death*. The ads screamed, "See mighty warriors attack each other with the most deadly weapons ever developed; their bare hands!" My favorite part of the movie was when the good guy reached into the chest of the bad guy so quickly and with such precision, that he had a moment to show the bad guy his own beating heart before that bad guy hit the ground. Now, honestly, what kid could possibly have asked for more on a Saturday afternoon? Clearly this five-finger thing stuck with me, and now that I'm (mostly) all grown up, I've used it and adapted it for business purposes.

Now, I'm not advocating that we want to rip anyone's heart out, and we certainly want all of our consumers and customers to live long, happy, prosperous lives so they can keep shopping, but every business owner would love to steal his customers' hearts and loyalties and make them her own. So, for the purpose of commerce, we'll soften that whole "death" thing and instead apply an old business term used to describe shoplifting: the five-finger discount. Larceny is better than murder, right? Since humans have five of these clever little appendages, they've long been used as a learning tool, so we'll stick with it.

The Five-Finger Discount, shown in Figure 4-1, describes five key strategies to attract your consumers, serve your customers, engage your customers in your products and services, optimize your business in search results, and build brand awareness. It's a simple plan—much of which began long before social commerce became so universal—but it's still a good business strategy and one that can easily increase sales and bind your customers

Figure 4-1

to you for more commerce. You may already be doing some of these things, but you're about to learn how to do them better and more effectively.

The Five-Finger strategies are as follows:

1. Sales funnel
2. Customer relationship management (CRM)
3. User-generated content (UGC)
4. Search engine optimization (SEO)
5. Brand awareness

THE FIRST FINGER: THE SALES FUNNEL

The elements of the sales funnel haven't changed in years. You will have to explore each level of this funnel if you're going to achieve your goal of attracting and keeping your customers. But as you'll soon see, the application of the sales funnel is much different than it used to be.

The levels of the sale funnel are the following:

- Awareness
- Interest
- Consideration
- Preference
- Purchase
- Up-sell
- Cross-sell
- Loyalty

The challenge itself hasn't changed. If you want someone to buy something from you, you'll always have to make a case, or "pitch," for why they should need or want whatever it is you sell. How you complete this process and navigate the sales funnel is now entirely different.

For example, before the dawn of e-commerce and the arrival of social commerce, merchants had a limited number of ways to attract their consumers. Advertising had three main channels: TV, radio, and print. You could also rent a billboard or buy some movie advertising, but TV, radio, and print were the main ways of getting your product in front of your consumers. Of course, TV offered the greatest opportunity to reach the largest number of people.

Before the days of cable TV—yes, many of us are old enough to remember that far back—there were generally three main TV networks. In local areas there may have been a public broadcast station or a couple of local outlets, but TV viewing was left to whatever happened to be on the channel at any given time. If you placed an ad on a major TV network, tens of millions of people might view it. Now, most of us have cable outlets that give us close to a thousand stations. Internet TV provides thousands more, and YouTube has joined the fray by offering virtually countless numbers of other viewing options. What about commercials? Well, many of us don't watch or listen to them at all. If you don't use a digital video recorder to capture your favorite shows and speed through the ads, I'm willing to bet you still watch TV with that little device in your hands—a remote—that allows us to quiet the commercials or flip channels to avoid them. Skipping through ads on TV is a more proactive way to *watch* entertainment, but it makes it much harder for you, as a business, to attract consumers with your brand message.

Don't even get me started on print and radio advertising. Magazine after magazine has switched to electronic-only format, and newspapers all over the country are shutting their doors. You can still place ads in both these outlets, but it's a lot more likely that, in 2014, those ads will be delivered electronically via the Internet. And radio advertising is equally anemic. Why should any of us listen to radio ads when we can carry our whole private music collection on a tiny player that fits inside our pockets? And we haven't even looked at all the other ways we get distracted today. We can spend our time with iPads, iPods, iPhones, smartphones, gaming systems, YouTube, Facebook, and a dozen other new media. Our attention spans have been fragmented by the plethora of choices we have about how we will spend our free time.

The old sales funnel was broad at the top and narrow at the bottom (see Figure 4-2). That's because the old outlets for making your pitch—for making your customers aware of your products—reached a wide audience composed of a variety of different people who didn't have many other choices. Still, capturing that customer and turning him into a lifelong devotee of your products and services was difficult. That's why the top of the old sales funnel was broad and the bottom was narrow. Once you reached your customer and convinced her to come in and shop with you, it was time to work on the bottom of the funnel. We all want to increase our profits by up-selling or cross-selling, but getting your customer to spend more than she intended to spend wasn't easy in the traditional model, and this is what both

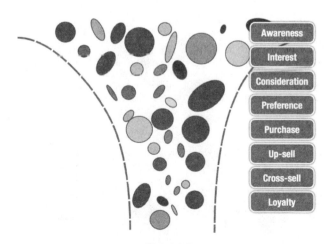

Figure 4-2

up-selling and cross-selling involve. Brand loyalty was also difficult to achieve, because those large and captive TV viewing audiences were always being pitched to by others selling products not only similar to yours but also products that claimed to be new and improved.

The Funnel Has Flipped

The sales cycle we experience today differs from this classic sales funnel. The elements are exactly the same, but the entire funnel has been turned on its head, and now that it's upside down, it's upside down for good. You're going to have to work a lot harder to reach a much smaller number of potential customers (see Figure 4-3). We have so many different forms of media vying for our attention now that even the three main TV networks struggle to gain the viewership they used to enjoy. The most popular TV show on the air today isn't likely to have anywhere near the regular viewership of the number one show as it held that spot in 1972, for example. In that year, *All in the Family* was the top-rated show. An estimated 67 million people all sat down

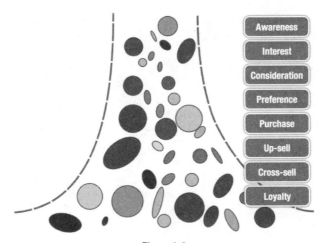

Figure 4-3

at the same time and watched it, according to an article written by Brandon Gutman for Forbes.com. Viewers all had to sit down at the same time because they had no other way to capture the show, and if they weren't ready to watch when it aired, they could only hope to catch it the next summer in reruns. Today, according to Gutman, five or six broadcast networks *combined* don't achieve that number of viewers. *American Idol* averages about 21 million viewers and *Modern Family* gets about 14 million. You will never be able to use TV advertising as the main way to reach your customers and achieve the same results once possible.

Change Is Good

Making your sales pitch can be challenging in today's multi-channel world. The good news is that once you do capture the attention of your King Consumers, the up-selling and cross-selling—the wide part of the funnel today—gets much easier. Now it isn't hard to up- or cross-sell once you've got the customer's interest; you can do either on your website or in the shopping cart. Up until the final push of a button that seals the sale, we can offer our customers accessories or items similar to the ones we know have drawn their interest and recommend products that interested others who made a similar purchase. A common guy like me, a small business owner, can do this without extra staff, because technology makes it a snap to work alone.

THE SECOND FINGER: CUSTOMER RELATIONSHIP MANAGEMENT

Customer relationship management (CRM) is especially important to online sales. In the physical world, you can build relationships with your customers by remembering their names, their favorite products, even their favorite colors. You might find yourself ordering products to sell specifically because you know a handful of your customers will want them. In e-commerce, this customer relationship management is more complicated, but it's still an achievable goal. You'll find getting to know your customers as people and allowing them to know you, too, will result in increased sales. Let's look at CRM across the whole life cycle you'll share with a customer.

Your customer's life cycle begins the first time he buys something from you and it ends the last time he makes a purchase. Your goal through CRM is twofold: Extend the life cycle while simultaneously increasing the frequency of transactions during that life cycle. Think about it. If you estimate your average customer will shop with you for about a year before moving on to wanting something else and will purchase from you three times within that year, you have a baseline to begin improving sales. If, over the course of that single year, you can get that one customer to shop and buy from you five times instead of three, you've nearly doubled your profit from only one customer. Apply that formula across many customers and your sales numbers will multiply.

Social media is a great tool for forming lasting relationships with your King Consumers. Even online, people shop with and buy from other people. Most of us prefer to buy from people we know and trust. Through CRM you can show your customers the person behind your business, which is sure to make them feel more comfortable buying from you. Letting your customers view you as human and viewing them that way, too, will enable you to build synergy with them, similar to what shopkeepers in the physical world do. Once you've established this synergy, your customers can tell you what they'd like to see added to your inventory, and you can tell them about what is going on in your business. You can keep them informed about upcoming sales and the new inventory items you will be adding to your line. You can share company goals that you are working toward and enlist their suggestions about the best ways to reach them. You can also target specific news, information, or product marketing to your customers, because they are much more receptive to these messages when coming from someone they know, like, and trust.

The social bond you've created with them is going to keep them checking your site and coming back for more product. Take the time to build the relationship, and they'll have no other reason to look for anyone else the next time they want to buy something that you sell. In this way, you'll also uncover some precious nuggets. From solid customer relationships come your best advocates for more sales. This bond is also likely to be something they share in their own social media circles, which in turn spreads your social commerce campaign even farther along than you could have on your own. We learned in Chapter 2 that Consumer Kings don't shop based on facts as much as they do opinion. Every customer who leaves your site with a positive opinion is a potential candidate to become an opinion leader when it comes to the products that you sell.

THE THIRD FINGER: USER GENERATED CONTENT

The first customer who leaves you feedback or writes a review or tells her social media friends about an interaction with you and your business has created a piece of user generated content (UGC). These opinions, observations, and remarks can be some of the most powerful bits of promotion available on the web. It's important, as a retailer, that you pay attention to and embrace the remarks your customers make, because they offer you a gold mine of market research that once cost good money to attain. You need to know specifically

- what they are saying;
- in what context they are saying it;
- to whom they are saying it; and
- what the sentiments are behind the words.

It's very important for you to be open and receptive to your customers' comments, whether good or bad. Actually, looking at the negative comments may be your best option for learning more about operating your business and improving your service. It's easy to take negative comments personally, but if you can get past the temptation to overreact to criticism, the negative comments can be your best friends. If someone is always telling you that everything you do is terrific, it may help boost your ego, but it won't motivate you to strive to do more and strive to do better. So keep in mind that UGC—even when negative—is the third finger, but that doesn't mean it's the middle one. So don't act like it is.

Think of your UGC as a free and ongoing focus group, only better. The standard format for a focus group is an artificial construction. People are culled and put together in a room where they know other people are watching and observing them. It's an environment where everyone knows exactly who is seeking information about what. The fact that it's observed means it isn't necessarily accurate. Thanks to social commerce you can have an ongoing focus group where you get genuine user feedback from real people who are really using your products in real time. These are concrete results in a real environment, and your King Consumer may never even know you are there and paying attention.

♠ BREAKING **THE ICE**

UGC Is a Text-based Phenomenon

It may seem UGC can only be found in text format. It's still tempting, even after all these years, to consider feedback on eBay or reviews on Amazon as the best spots to find out what your customers are thinking, but it's just not true. You can find UGC in text, but also in video and photos. Think about it. If your customer buys a new camera, it's pretty likely that at least some photos taken with that model and make of camera already appear on somebody's Facebook page somewhere, and there you can see who is using the product and how they feel about it. No question. If you sell toys, you're going to find video and photos of somebody's precious grandchild using your products. There are lots of ways to get information about your customers and products and text is only one of those ways.

Okay, so just as you shouldn't assume all input will come at you in the form of words, you also shouldn't assume that you'll only find your products being discussed on people's Facebook pages, in snippets on Twitter, and in formal feedback and review areas. I personally find some of the best conversations about my products happening in the old-fashioned forums that have been part of the online experience since it began, even before the Internet was named. These groups and forums could be on Facebook, but there are a lot of other places where you'll find them, too. For example, if you sell coffee products there are *dozens* of chat rooms specific to coffee. The chat board at CoffeeForums.com has more than 25,150 members and fifty-seven thousand posts about nothing but coffee-related topics. Here's a community that is very active and passionate about coffee.

I find some of the deepest and most poignant conversations occur in groups and forums. Plus, if you're reading for observational purposes only, you don't have to announce who you are and what you sell. You can simply use these conversations to learn about what your King Consumers are saying about you and your products. Believe me when I tell you they are talking about it, and you owe it to yourself to know what they are saying. Once you get the lay of the land, you can be more direct. Trust me. If you want to know what your customers are saying about you and your products, find where they chat, and go ahead and ask them. They'll be happy to share their opinions with you along with the other members of their groups.

And how will you find where your King Consumers are doing all this chatting and sharing? Nobody can answer that specifically for you. You are the one most likely to uncover these places, because you're the one most devoted to your products. The exact locations will become apparent to you only with monitoring, searching, and researching. It's a good thing you like all three of those!

♦ ICE MAKER

Use Google to Stay Alert

You should already have Google Alerts set up to detect the words your King Consumers are using. You do have Google Alerts set up, right? I know that this is an old-school tool at this point, but it's still a great one. Google Alerts is a program that will send you e-mail updates based on whatever search terms you decide are relevant. You can set it up to receive updates about your search terms on a weekly, daily, or real-time basis. You can also set it up to include only news or blogs or even video. Of course, you'll want to leave the default setting at "everything." That way you won't miss a single mention of your business, products, or brand. This is especially useful if you find someone who has made negative comments about your business, because you can proactively get in touch with that customer to try and resolve the issue, even before she's brought it to your attention. Talk about customer service! So, if you don't have Google Alerts set up already, chose a couple of your best keywords and go set it up now. Go ahead. I'll wait here for you to get back.

THE FOURTH FINGER: SEARCH ENGINE OPTIMIZATION

Search engine optimization, or SEO, isn't new, and most people who operate an e-commerce business have been thinking about it for years. I'm going to bring you into the second half of the second decade of the twenty-first century, so that you can go beyond the basic information you'll find all over the web. If you've never worked at all to optimize your site for search engines, you can read all about it through Google's SEO Starter Guide. (Search

Google for it.) But I'm going to assume you've at least tried to bring your business up higher in search results.

I see three basic best practices for anyone wanting to optimize search results, and they start with the way you title your website.

1. Be sure your target keyword phrase is part of your website's title page. For example, if you sell pet supplies, choose a domain name such as WorldsBestPetSupplies.com, which will automatically list you higher up on the search page whenever someone is looking for pet supplies online.

2. Include an optimized title meta tag. A meta tag is an HTML (hypertext markup language) tag that gives information about a web page. They're different from normal HTML tags, because they don't have any effect on how a page displays. They provide information that includes which keywords represent the page's content, and search engines use this information when building indices. So, rather than stuffing your title with keywords, incorporate your most important keyword phrase for the page into your title. For example, World's Best Pet Supplies Online might be a good title to use.

3. Include an optimized description meta tag, too. As long as you're working on meta tags, be sure to put some in your descriptions. They should contain your web page's title and a compelling reason or a call to action that will entice people to visit your site. For example, "World's Best Pet Supplies offers shoppers the highest quality products, fastest shipping, and greatest customer service on the Internet." Then you can add the names of the brands you carry.

The number one benefit of social media, in my opinion, is how effectively it boosts SEO. Social media ranks well in Google and Bing searches, so comments and content posted on sites like Facebook and Twitter will improve your position in searches.

Today, SEO is no longer only about searching, but also about finding; it allows people to find your business even when they are just browsing the online places where they hang out. So, if you add social bookmarking sites like Reddit, StumbleUpon, and others to your SEO mix, you will see expanded results and improved positioning.

ICE MAKER

Write About It

Google absolutely loves blogs and ranks them very, very highly. It actually stores an index for blogs and shows new content added to those blogs very quickly. This gives you an edge over your competitors who aren't blogging to improve SEO. When you are creating fresh content relevant to your topic, Google will use that content and position you higher in that topical search category. So, even if you've never thought of yourself as a writer, blogging will help you rank higher. You don't have to be Hemingway, you just have to provide good content relevant to your customers. So get started! Don't worry. You'll be getting a lot of help from me with that in just a few chapters.

If you're already blogging, be sure to make your posts evergreen so that the content doesn't expire. Also, go ahead and include a few links, but *do not* overdo this. You want people to notice that, in coming to you, they found good information and not just a sales pitch. If you respect them in this regard, they'll respect you, too, and be much more likely to track your blog and visit again. Stumped for a topic? To continue with our pet-supply example, you could begin with "Five Tips for Grooming Your Dog." Your consumers will love you for it. Plus, remember, you don't have to write a new posting every day. If you update your blog as little as once a week, you should see results.

If you're feeling a little nervous about all that writing, remember text isn't the only medium you can use to impress your customers. I've had fantastic results on YouTube, and as you'll see in the second half of this book, making videos can actually be a lot of fun. Years ago I created a video on YouTube showing people how to fold a bandana. I was getting a lot of requests from my international customers asking me how to fold a bandana so they could look like Tupac Shakur. It was simple enough for me to create a video demonstrating several easy techniques for getting the look my customers wanted. I posted it in YouTube's "How-to" area to see what would happen: That simple little video recorded with very few frills has been viewed more than 250,000 times! Actually, that number isn't accurate, because all the people who read this book before you have gone to check it out. It cost me nothing to create. I spent a few minutes doing it, and the results have been simply fantastic. Why? Because it gets indexed every time someone searches for a video showing them how to tie a bandana.

THE FIFTH FINGER: BRAND AWARENESS

Everyone talks about building their brand across the World Wide Web. In the early years of social commerce, when people were told to begin promoting their businesses on social media sites, most of them went about their branding all wrong.

In the Old West, cowboys had to brand their cattle. We've all seen a cowboy poised on top of a galloping horse chasing after a horrified calf with a lasso. Our cowboy hero would get close enough to capture the little guy, and then he'd wrestle the calf to the ground, hog-tie its legs, and hold it still while another cowboy seared the rancher's brand onto its flesh with a hot branding iron, so that everyone could easily see which rancher that soon-to-be fully grown calf belonged to.

That is what I see people doing in social commerce all the time. They want to wrestle their customers to the ground where they can't move away and then just hammer them with the message of their brand. I don't think this is the best way to do your branding. Remember, you only get one chance when using social commerce to turn people off by spamming them with your message. If you spam them, people won't trust the brand you're trying to build, but they won't trust you, either. You've just made it clear to them that you came to social media to profit from them. That makes you noise and your consumers won't want to become your customers.

Instead, I consider branding to be very simply defined. Your brand is what people think and say about you when you're not there to observe. That's your personal brand. It's also the same concept with your business. It's how people talk about your products and services when you're not participating in the conversation. Making sure consumers say good things can be summed up with the Five C's of Branding:

1. Clear messaging: As with the story of the bumblebee in Chapter 3, your branding has to have a clear message, and it has to be small. Just as the pollen is small enough not to overwhelm the bee, your message has to be small enough so your customers can go from place to place and deposit your brand.
2. Credibility: Bring out your persona. Give the consumers the feeling and emotion of your brand, and let your consumers feel attached to it. Creating credibility builds loyalty and loyalty means repeat business.
3. Connection: Create a sincere connection between your consumers and your brand. You are the connection with those consumers and through you the consumer will be connected with your brand.
4. Create loyalty: Begin finding those customers in your sales funnel who can actually be turned into brand loyalists. Once you do, those customers will create user generated content (UGC) around your brand That UGC will spread across

their networks, too. Once you find them, you're ready for the final C.

5. Convert: Now you've converted them into brand advocates. They'll take your branding efforts into places where you may not have thought to go.

As you go about building your brand, it's once again important to take the time to listen to and observe your King Consumers. There are very few rules in social networks, but these online communities rely upon people, and people don't like it when you disrespect their communities. If you start your branding efforts off on the wrong foot, it can be very difficult to recover. It's very important that you take the time you need to learn about the places that you want to promote your brand. Don't make the mistake of assuming you can figure it out as you go along. It doesn't work that way, and this is one area of social commerce where you can't afford to make too many early mistakes.

USING THE FIVE-FINGER DISCOUNT GIVES YOU ONE MIGHTY FIST

Now that you understand the Five Fingers, let's discuss a few examples of how you will combine them and put them into service to achieve your goals. Like any other set of tools, you won't necessarily use them all every time you set out to accomplish a task. You'll mix and match them according to whatever it is you set out to do. For example, if you want to improve your website's ranking in search results, you'd use the Third and Fourth Fingers. Of course you'd focus on SEO, but you'd also work with UGC to boost your rankings as your King Consumers post, blog, or tweet about your products and services. To boost your brand awareness, you'd make use of the Fifth Finger, but you'd also be sure to focus on the Second Finger, customer relationship management and, once again, the Third Finger.

But no matter what your objective, make sure you clearly understand what it is you're setting out to do. It's not good enough to simply say, "I want to sell more stuff." Really? What business owner doesn't want to sell more stuff? I know I do, and so does everyone else who uses social commerce. That goal is way too broad to be effective. Before you go about sticking your Five Fingers into everyone's faces, identify two or three very clear objectives and then select and combine two or three of those Five Fingers to work toward your objectives.

SUMO LESSON

I was working with an Australian client, Deals Direct (DealsDirect .com.au), which brought me in to talk to its social commerce marketing team. The task at hand was to answer the question, "How do we get people to be more aware of our product and selling more of our product?" I wanted to work with a single or SKU (stock-keeping unit), so I could take the principle I wanted to share and expand it to other areas of the business. I decided to use a stop-snoring spray it was selling.

My first task was to figure out how people were searching for products like the snoring spray. I used Wordtracker, a free keyword-suggestion tool, and the first phrase I tried was "stop snoring." Wordtracker showed us how people were using these keywords; how they were searching the web with them. I got back results that included about twenty different things. I focused on three or four of the top results: I used "how to stop snoring," "tips to stop snoring," "products to stop snoring," and "stop snoring surgery."

Now the first three terms show what people are actually typing into their Google searches. If I create content that answers these questions, those people will see that content in response to their searches. I will answer exactly what they are looking for, and that will rank higher in Google. People will spend more time on my site reading those tips because they're relevant to those searches. That equals three great blog posts that I can create about snoring. I can come up with a top stop snoring list of suggestions and at the end I can put links to both our site and to the spray.

At the end of the blog postings, I recommended to Deals Direct that we give readers the reward: Here's how you actually stop snoring. You use our spray. This is a really creative way to use the information for marketing. I chose the phrase "stop snoring surgery," because a lot of people were searching for it. Now, my client doesn't offer surgery, of course, but think about it. Before deciding to go under the knife to stop your snoring, wouldn't you at least consider trying the $9.99 solution of a bottle of snoring spray? Of course you would! So I think creating a little bit of content around that surgery will result in sales. It will let people know that, hey, before you subject yourself to the pain and expense of surgery, try this product first. Who in his right mind would skip over that?

I took my results to Direct's marketing team for an aha! moment about how they could leverage the specific wording and questions their King Consumers were using on Google and social media. I showed them that instead of just jumping into the conversation willy-nilly, they should take the information I'd gathered and create full blog-type content. This content would be evergreen on their e-commerce website—always relevant, timely, and constantly working to sell their snoring spray.

That's a Rap!

✔ I understand the Five Fingers that will allow me to steal the hearts of my King Consumers.

✔ I see exactly how the traditional sales funnel has been flipped upside down, and I know it's not likely to be flipped back to what it was anytime soon.

✔ I will use social media to engage with my customers and extend the lifecycle during which they will shop with me.

✔ I have some strategies that will help me embrace my customers' comments, both positive and negative.

✔ I've set up Google Alerts so I can track what my customers are saying about my products and services.

✔ I have some great ideas about how I can use SEO to improve my rankings in search results of all types.

✔ If I ever engaged in spamming my customers, I'll never do it again.

✔ I know how to combine my Five Fingers to achieve specific objectives and create a powerful fist that will help increase my sales and profits.

CHAPTER 5

A Good Name Is Better Than Diamonds

"If you do build a great experience, customers tell each other about that. Word of mouth is very powerful."

—Jeff Bezos

When it comes to social commerce, Mom was right. Your reputation is easily broken, and once broken, it can be very challenging to repair. In 2014, not only can your reputation take the usual hits, but in the world of social media, anybody can say anything about you from anywhere in the world and keep it up for weeks, even months. Then, their social networks can pick up the insults and spread them even farther. Let's take a minute to think about that. Chew it around for a few minutes. Swish it around in your mouth so you can get a good taste of it. Okay, now, spit it out. How'd that feel? Not so good, right? Let's look at a real disaster that struck a small business when a cyberbully decided to take action.

David Isermate owns a local eatery in La Jolla, California. He and his wife, Elle, had been in corporate jobs all their lives. In his mid-forties, David was at the top of his field in personal real estate. As he saw the markets begin to slip, late in 2007, he pulled back on his real estate business and put all of his energies toward fulfilling a lifelong dream. David always wanted to own and operate his own restaurant. By the middle of 2008, when the real estate market was crashing toward the Great Recession, his restaurant was ready to launch.

After navigating a tough first two years through a very bad economy, David and his restaurant came out the other side. Success was his, and by the end of 2011, Elle had left her corporate job to work with David and run the front of the house. David and Elle were doing great things and had a steady stream of customers and patrons. Elle made a special point to check the restaurant reviews every day, and their hard work was paying off. Everything was fantastic! Their customers gave great feedback about how much they enjoyed eating at David's dream restaurant. That is until one day in particular.

David says that he will *never* forget that day. It was the week after the July Fourth party he and his family had at the restaurant. A customer came in to the establishment and already seemed a little "inebriated" according to Elle. He was not overly so, but you could tell he had a buzz going on, for sure. He had a young lady with him and Elle seated the two at table 14. The server that night, Angela, said that after ordering a bottle of wine the "gentleman" started getting a little fresh with her. He was actually flirting with the waitstaff right there in front of his date. Angela was a little miffed but did her best to pay no attention to him. By the time the first course was served, the wine was gone and a second bottle was on its way, and this is where things went bad.

Angela was serving the main course when the man grabbed her in a very inappropriate manner. She put the food down, spun around, and told him to *stop it*. She then ran to the kitchen for support. Flustered and clearly upset, she told David about what happened and what she had been subjected to from the customer at table 14—from now on known as Mr. Asshat. By the time David got to the dining area, he was shocked to see the man arguing with a guy from table 12! Now things had gone way too far. Mr. Asshat had to go. David and a couple of waitstaff broke up the confrontation before it got physical, and David immediately escorted Mr. Asshat to the door. He and his date left without incident, and David thought that would be the end of it.

The next day, David and Elle were going through their routines at work. David was getting things ready for service and Elle was checking the restaurant reviews. She noticed, for the first time, a one-star rating on one of the restaurant review sites. The review spoke about the poor service and the terrible food. After years of great reviews this concerned her, not in an alarming way, but enough to make her match up the food discussed in the review with the tickets from the night before. Lo and behold there it was. The two entrees that the reviewer was complaining about were the same two from Mr. Asshat's order. The man who had been drinking his meal, without ever actually eating the main course before being evicted, was now leaving bad remarks about the food and the service. No surprise, since clearly, the guy was a complete jerk. She showed the review to David. They talked about the bad scene from the night before and decided to just ignore it.

Unfortunately, Mr. Asshat was *not* your ordinary jerk, and he wasn't in the mood to ignore anything. The next day three more negatives showed up for the restaurant on three more review sites. The day after that there were even *more*! Mr. Asshat had gone directly into cyberbully mode. He was bombing review sites about the restaurant all over the web. David and Elle suddenly had friends, family, and customers asking about it. The reviews had spread clearly beyond anything David and Elle could have anticipated. So, how could one man cause so much havoc?

I wish I could tell you that this is an unusual story, but sorry, it's not. This type of behavior happens all the time for businesses large and small. Both brick-and-mortar and online stores have to deal with reputation management. That means you do, too. You'll get comments, both positive and negative, and this is where the information in this chapter applies. If Mr. Asshat decides to shop with you, you'll be well-prepared to deal with him.

FEEDBACK AND REVIEWS

In Chapter 2 you learned that the King Consumer is not more empowered in this new world of electronic opinion than you are. That's the good news. The bad news, as you've just seen, is that an unreasonable and vindictive King can make for a really lousy week at work. To make the system work effectively for you, you'll need to first take a good hard look at the system itself.

Back in the early days, when Amazon was primarily a place on the web to buy books, the company instituted a simple review system. By nature, people who buy books like to discuss them, review them, recommend them to their friends. Originally, Amazon's review system was a simple way for readers and customers to share opinions about what they were buying and reading. The reviews were all listed chronologically, and the simple system worked well—for a while. Like so many simple and good ideas, the Amazon community quickly outgrew the review system.

It's one thing to list all reviews chronologically when there are no more than a couple of dozen. Someone devoted to finding out about a book would be likely to scroll through a page or two of reviews to get all the positive and negative feedback about a particular title. It's an entirely different story when a book, a popular one for example, garners several hundreds or even thousands of reviews. At that point, it becomes less likely that reviews beyond the latest couple of dozen will matter. Usually even devoted readers won't go through the trouble of reading all the reviews, and some of the best ones may have been written long enough in the past to have scrolled off.

When the Amazon marketplace expanded to include all types of products and third-party sellers, the whole chronological review system was no longer sustainable yet, at the same time, it became more popular than ever. Many people check the Amazon reviews for products, even if they don't plan to make the purchase on Amazon. As we all know, King Consumers want to vet their decisions through the opinions of other shoppers who have already purchased the products and are using them.

That's when the people at Amazon made a brilliant change to the simple review system. They allowed shoppers on the site to review the reviews! With a simple and discreet button, the company began to ask people, "Was this review helpful to you?" Notice, the question isn't "Do you agree?" It isn't, "Was this review good." It only asks how helpful a particular customer has found this particular review. Since the addition of this question and two simple buttons to reply Yes or No with, reviews are no longer listed in the order in which they were posted. Now, the most helpful reviews are listed first, which includes the top three good reviews and the top three negative reviews. "We can clearly see that promoting the most helpful reviews has increased sales in these categories by 20 percent. One out of every five customers decides to complete the purchase because of the strength of the reviews," wrote Amazon's Jared Spool in a 2009 article for *User Interface Engineering.* Jared estimated the review rating system was responsible for several billion dollars' worth of new revenue for Amazon.

So, as you can see, reviews both positive and negative can boost your bottom line, too. That is if you know how to cope with the "bad" ones. But first let's gain some perspective.

MY MOMMY ISN'T 100 PERCENT HAPPY WITH ME

Sad to say, but true. My mommy made me; she pushed me out of her own body. No one on earth loves me, worries about me, cares for me the way she does. It doesn't matter what I do, she'll always love me. I was her first-born child, and my spot in her life is set in cement. This still doesn't mean she's always happy with me. Sometimes she's actually pretty dissatisfied with me. Admit it. Yours probably feels the same way about you. If we can't please our own moms 100 percent of the time, why on earth would we stress over pleasing total strangers with every transaction we make? I came to e-commerce the way so many others did, by selling on eBay. In those early days, so many of us were exploring eBay as nothing more than a hobby. Once I got serious about building an online business, I started to participate in the seller communities. That's when I started to notice some odd behavior.

Sellers were obsessed with maintaining a 100 percent positive feedback rating. Forget 99 percent, because that represented a failure of some sort. As a matter of fact, my fellow eBay sellers were so obsessed with that number, they would do anything to keep from getting even one negative comment from a buyer. Some of them would hound buyers to remove a negative. Some would turn to eBay in hopes of getting that comment nullified—good luck with that. I knew sellers who offered to refund the entire price of a purchase if the unhappy customer would just remove the negative comment. Some even went so far as to threaten their own customers with retribution! I have to admit, I got sucked into this frenzy, too, but only for about the first one hundred transactions. Then I saw how silly it was.

Let's look at the numbers. Out of one hundred transactions, only about half of your customers will even bother to leave feedback. Now you're looking at the opinions of only about 50 percent of your customers. If one person in that group leaves you a negative comment, your feedback rating goes down to 98 percent, a failure according to many eBay sellers. Now, I'm not saying your online reputation isn't important. Of course it is. Your SEO can falter with poor ratings. Your reputation in the online community is your wallet, and just like your wallet, you need to protect it. But at the same time, you'll be happier and healthier if you accept that you aren't going to be 100 percent perfect.

Fortunately, online commerce has matured to a point where customers understand that there are pros and cons to every transaction. When they see a 100 percent rating today, in 2014, it seems suspicious. It's too perfect. You'll find that a 99 percent rating is more believable. It's more in keeping with the imperfections of life in general and transacting business online in particular.

As a matter of fact, 99.5 percent positive feedback means you're probably paying more attention to the other parts of your business that really are more important. The difference won't affect your sell-through rate at all. Your efforts are better spent offering easy shipping and return options, or concentrating on your pricing policies, or working on the overall look and feel of your sites, your pictures and descriptions. These are real elements that *will* result in greater sell-through rates.

Nothing in life is perfect. We're not 100 percent satisfied with anything: not our bodies, not our marriages, not our democracy, not our choices in our elected officials. Even in nature there are no perfect circles. If nature can't get things to be 100 percent satisfactory, why would we humans think this is a valid goal? So, absolutely, do whatever you can to safeguard your online reputation, but at the same time, chill out. You're never going to please every customer in every way with every transaction. Everybody isn't going to love you, and they're damn well not going to love you more than your less-than-100-percent-satisfied mom.

ICE MAKER

Ask and You Shall Receive

As you saw in the previous illustration, it only takes one negative comment out of fifty responses to drop your feedback rating on eBay from 100 percent positive to 98 percent. Although you're no longer going to obsess about that golden 100, you still want to maintain a good positive rating. One of the ways to do this is to actually solicit feedback from your customers. That's user generated content (UGC) you can use.

Create a little comment request card to slip into every package you ship. Make it simple, but ask your customer to be in touch if there are any issues with the order, and give them simple ways to contact you directly. This way, if you have an unhappy shopper, you can provide this person with great customer service before he goes public with his discontent. On the other hand, if you make your request personable and friendly, the satisfied customers will be more inclined to take a minute to leave you a positive response. They understand how the system works, too. If you can get seventy out of one hundred customers to respond, that single negative comment will have a much smaller overall impact on your business.

POLISH THOSE NEGATIVES

When you do get a negative review or comment, it's time to jump into scramble mode to make sure the impact of that response is contained. Fortunately, we'll discuss some solid tools for dealing with them. Before you go from zero to ballistic, be honest. Does this customer have a valid point? Sometimes we get so bogged down in the details of our businesses from our own perspectives, that we forget they may seem quite different from our customers' points of view. Some of our best business adaptations can evolve from the comments we get from our customers. They are the proven experts when it comes to our policies and processes. Before you get too worked up, ask yourself if this comment or review offers any insights you can use to make your business or service better. If not, then by all means, get busy making the best of a bad review, but remember it's not personal, so even though it feels that way, don't take it personally. Losing your temper will only escalate a confrontation with a customer, and you don't want to turn someone with a problem into your own personal version of Mr. Asshat.

The Magic Words

The first step in any disagreement between merchant and King is to invoke three simple but magical words: I am sorry. Now, before you protest that you're not really sorry and your King is being a jerk, take a step back. I'm not saying you should use this phrase to accept responsibility or agree with a disgruntled King. I'm saying use it for your own benefit. It's pretty hard to stay angry with someone who is willing to apologize. In the tens of thousands of transactions I've completed throughout the years, I've met my share of angry people. Saying a simple "I'm sorry" usually cools the fires in their bellies. I haven't once said, "I'm sorry we screwed up" unless of course we have actually screwed up.

Here is a list of apologies I've used in the past:

I am sorry that you're unhappy …
I am sorry to hear that your package did not arrive …
I am sorry to learn you gave us the wrong address …
I am sorry you left the package out in the rain and it got ruined …
I am sorry that you thought fuchsia was green …
I am sorry you think that I'm stupid …

I don't care what the problem is. I always start with these three little words, combined with whatever the particular issue is. All I'm saying is that I empathize with the customer and her concerns, and I'm willing to listen to the issues my King Consumers bring to me. Do this first, and you have a chance to prevent negative comments before they begin. You also get the chance to hear from a King who may actually have a legitimate issue that was your fault. Handling complaints in a respectful and positive manner often turns a potential adversary into a cheerleader. That's the magic of those three little words.

⬆ BREAKING THE ICE

Extend Your Return Period

I know, I know. I just finished telling you to apologize even if you don't want to, and now I'm telling you to give your customers more time to return whatever it is you sell for a full refund. How many horrible suggestions can I fit into one single chapter? Well, as you'll see, just like saying "I am sorry" works like magic, so does extending your return period. Trust me.

I paid a visit to Zappos, an online merchant with probably the best customer service reputation of them all. They have a one-year return policy. One whole year to return whatever you bought that didn't suit you. This seems extreme, but you can't quarrel with success. When I came back home, I changed my return policy to "90 days full refund." This one change didn't add a single additional refund. No one has ever tried to return something seventy-five days after buying it. The new policy did, however, increase our number of buyers by about 5 to 7 percent. We didn't change anything else, just the refund period. Our refunds actually went down, and I think I know why now.

If you tell someone she has seven days to return an item she isn't happy about, this deadline stays high on her to-do list. She knows this is something she has to take care of right away if she wants her money back. Now, humans will always be humans. Tell her she has ninety days to get a full refund, and she's likely to stick that item away until she gets around to running the errand. You've taken the urgency out of her task. Humans, by nature, tend to procrastinate, and you've made it possible for her to operate by way of human nature. If she's really unhappy, you'll get it back in a week or so. But usually the transaction becomes less important to her with each passing day.

With a seven-day refund policy, you're likely to hear from her ten days or even a couple of weeks later. She'll have a whole list of excuses for why she didn't return it on time: "I was away on business"; "I went on vacation"; "My kids were sick, and I couldn't get out to mail it." Becoming adversarial is always possible with someone who is trying everything she can to get her money back, even though she didn't follow your policy. If you give her ninety days, and she realizes on day 95 that she never got around to sending it back, she knows the fault is hers. Your policies were perfectly reasonable, but she just didn't get around to it. Her dissatisfaction won't be nearly as important to her three months after it first happened. She can't return it, and it's *not* your fault! Give it a try and see for yourself. I think you'll be amazed by how well it works.

Remember Who Your Audience Really Is

No matter where your customers comment about your products and services, those comments will reside where the whole world can see them. Your job is, of course, to try to correct any mistakes and smooth ruffled feathers, but it goes beyond that. Your reputation in a world of social commerce is probably more dependent on how you handle problems than it is on how you handle transactions that run smoothly. If your dissatisfied King posts a negative comment on a social network, that comment can go around the world and back again before you get done with your breakfast. So, your job is twofold. Absolutely, do your best to contain the damage, but at the same time, take each comment as an opportunity to show everyone else in the "room" how you handle yourself and your customers. Your response should be 50 percent aimed at the disgruntled individual and 50 percent aimed at everyone else.

That's all the more reason you need to act like a damned professional when you deal with your Kings. They're being judged by their peers, but so are you. Let them show their true colors while you focus on presenting yourself in the best light. Be sure to stay true to your values. Be professional with your language. Always explain what you can do, but never try to justify what you can't do. Don't even mention it. You don't want other potential customers focusing on your deficiencies. You want them witnessing your best practices. Preparing in advance can help you with this.

Be sure you know in advance where you're willing to draw the line and where you're not willing to let others cross that line. You don't have to be held hostage by Mr. Asshat, but you also need to be sure no one following this angry exchange thinks you are responsible for it, or even contributing to it. You will be judged by how you respond. The more professionally you behave the more benefit you'll bring to your reputation. Once again, Mom was right. It is much easier to maintain a good reputation than it is to repair a bad one. Make sure whatever you do when relating to your customers makes you and your business look good. The more experience you gain dealing with these challenges, the more comfortable you'll be when facing that next unhappy King.

Be SMART

SMART is an acronym that will help you remember some basic steps for creating and cementing a solid positive reputation for yourself as a businessperson and your business as a place your Kings want to visit, and frequently.

S—Solicit feedback and comments for user generated content (UGC).
M—Magic words are "I am sorry ..."
A—An audience is watching you respond.
R—Real feedback beats a fake 100 percent positive ranking, every day.
T—Trust comes from consistent reputation management, so build it with each encounter.

Now, before we move into the next chapter, I thought you'd like to know how David and Elle's story ended. The couple and their staff at the restaurant had a really bad week after Mr. Asshat decided to stop by the eatery. They worried about the long-term effect of having such negative reviews marking their online reputation. Fortunately, they'd been working hard at running their place, and the regulars who came in were not happy to hear what had happened to their local eatery. Once David and Elle started sharing their story, their regular customers were more than happy to post reviews that put Mr. Asshat's work into perspective.

SUMO LESSON

I used to worry all the time about getting a negative comment on eBay. The sellers on that platform had me frightened to death that one bad comment would remove my 100 percent feedback. I did everything to keep my 100 percent. I even gave customers free items via refunds just to make them happy!

One day I ran into a true jackass who gave us the wrong delivery address. When he moved from his old place, he updated his address on PayPal, the main conduit for receiving electronic payments for eBay purchases, but neglected to update it on eBay. And because he placed his order on eBay, the system automatically defaulted to his eBay address as the delivery address. No amount of reasoning or explaining could make this guy change his opinion. After nearly two hundred positive feedbacks, I got my first permanent negative!

I thought the world was over and my sales would suffer dramatically. However, exactly the opposite happened. My sales the following week were actually higher than for the previous week. I won't say we got a boost from having our new 99.9 percent feedback rating, but it clearly didn't do us any harm. Plus, you can be damn sure I started to sleep easier every night, without the paranoia about what would happen if I got a single negative response. No harm, no foul, and my business did not suffer one bit.

Today I correct my mistakes just as diligently and provide the *best* service on the web. It is in our business DNA. However I no longer have to worry about Mr. Asshat or his companions. I can show them the door with confidence. I will never be held hostage by any client or customer, because I know that we are doing our best for every King Consumer who shops with us. That feels really good!

That's a Rap!

✔ In the world of social commerce, I will have to deal with feedback, both positive and negative.

✔ The success of my business does not rely on maintaining a spotless record.

✔ I will never please every King Consumer, so I won't waste too much energy trying to.

✔ I will solicit comments from my customers and make it easy for them to share their opinions.

✔ I will not take a negative comment personally, and I will never allow myself to publicly "fight" with a customer.

✔ I will use the magic words, "I am sorry ..."

✔ I will remember that my audience includes far more people than just the King Consumer I am trying to appease.

PART TWO

The Gravy—Social Commerce Strategy for the Top Social Sites

CHAPTER 6

Right Here, Write Now: Create Your **Social Commerce Strategy**

"Nothing is more destructive to a man than his own decisions ... choose wisely!"

—*John Lawson (moi!)*

As you're aware by now, there is a big difference between social media and social commerce. I am way more concerned with being good at business than I am with being good with social media. Everybody seems to want to rush off to all their favorite social networking sites and start talking. Fortunately, you're smarter than that and much better educated as we begin the second half of this book.

You know it's true. Most businesses have some sort of social media programs in place, but what you might not know is that most of them don't have any strategic plan for using social media at all. In a study published by the online magazine Social Media Examiner in May 2013, its founder, Michael A. Stelzner, reported that 86 percent of marketers consider social media to be important to their businesses and at least 88 percent of marketers want to know the best tactics and strategies to engage their customers in social media. This is a huge issue. It means nearly all business owners recognize social media is important to their businesses, so they're on social media. But even more of them recognize they're uncertain about how to effectively use the sites. This uncertainty makes strategic planning impossible. You already know it's not enough to just try to find your King Consumers. That's a beginning, but now it's time for you to decide and plan what you want social media to do for you once you find them. Without a plan, you'll have nothing of any value to share once you become part of the crowd. This is probably the number one reason why social media is failing for most business users. People rush to create an online presence without deciding what they want to do with it. Without a clear strategy, how will you know where to engage your King Consumers and what to do once you get there?

Maybe you're not surprised that so many business owners go rushing onto social media sites without a plan. You may have already done that yourself. If so, it will not surprise you to learn that these same people who put lots of effort into their "social media marketing" plans often don't bother to put measures in place that allow them to gather the data about how their efforts are actually working for them. Of course, they can't measure what they're doing. They didn't plan to do anything in particular, so how are they going to measure whether or not they accomplished it? You can't improve what you are not measuring, and you can't achieve what you haven't planned to do. This brings me to some good news and also a bit of bad news.

The good news is that you're not going to do this same bone-headed thing. You're going to know very clearly what you hope to achieve as you use social media to complete your social commerce plan. The bad news is that you're not going to get much farther here unless you sit down and do the strategic planning so many of your peers have decided to skip. No way. If you're going to make this trip with me, you're going to know how to plan it in advance. Now, actually "bad news" is an exaggeration. It's not exactly bad news. It's going to set you up to achieve real goals, and I've done my best to make it painless. I admit it's not fun, but it is necessary. Let's begin with a couple of pieces of wisdom.

Let me be the first one to tell you right now, there is no magic formula that every business should use to find the answers to their social commerce objectives. If someone comes to your door to sell you on social media and starts out spouting the averages, you can be sure they will do just that for your business—make it *average* at best. I want us to go way beyond the average. We want the super-fantastic-hyper-killing-it methods. Glad you picked up this book? Good. Nobody is going to care more about your business than you do, and nobody is going to understand the workings of your operation like you do. You *must* do this work yourself, no arguments.

Luckily for you, step-by-step instructions for how to use every single platform covered in this part of the book are not included. That would be an insult to you. All of these platforms are designed to be easy to navigate and use. I trust you will be able to figure the nuts and bolts out on your own. I'm here to help you with the "what" and "why." I have confidence you will handle the "how" part of it by yourself. Here's an analogy to keep in mind. Many people know how to use a hammer. What's to know? You basically swing it and make the head of the hammer hit the head of the nail. When working with my dad, he taught me that if I moved my hand down lower on the handle of the hammer it would work much better and hit the nails in faster. He did not tell me how to pick out a particular hammer. He showed me how to use any hammer more efficiently. That's what we're about to do. I am not going hammer shopping with you. We will not talk about how metal handles compare to wooden handles or any of the minutia of hammer technology. So I won't cover setting up a Facebook page or how to register for Twitter. That information is on the Help pages. You can get to them easily. And if hundreds of millions of people have already done it, I know for sure you can, too. You've come here to focus on learning how to position your hand on the handle so the fulcrum of your hammer swing is maximized for optimal nailing.

ICE MAKER

Take the Pareto Principle with You

Have you ever heard of the Pareto Principle? Its most common name is the 80/20 Rule. I find this rule is very applicable to social commerce, and you'll find it sprinkled throughout the rest of this book. I will use it to describe the way people are expected to interact on social media, and I will also apply it to the way business owners post content for their King Consumers. For now, just keep in mind that, for each of the social networks we're about to explore, your plan is to offer value 80 percent of the time and promote sales only 20 percent. This advice will help a lot as you build your social commerce strategy.

ASSESS YOURSELF

Just so you know the truth, I didn't begin my business with the kind of preplanning I'm asking you to do. I'm like so many e-commerce merchants. I never planned to be in business. Sure, I've always had a sense for the business hustle, but I'm a circumstantial entrepreneur. When I started selling on eBay, it was just for fun. By the time it turned into a real business, my partner and I were so busy trying to keep up that I didn't even take time to breathe, let alone really plan. I've learned over the years how important the planning step is, because I missed it!

Now my partner and I have a tradition. Every New Year's Eve we go to a great hotel. We have a party with all of our friends and enjoy the night. The next day, before we check out of the hotel, we find a quiet corner and plan what we want to accomplish in the year ahead. So do whatever you have to do to make this a good exercise. If it means you check into a nice hotel, go for it. It works for us. If you'd rather take to the park or the beach or your local coffee shop, do it. There's no right or wrong place to be as long as you're not skipping ahead to the next chapter by now.

First be honest with yourself about how many social media sites you are on, how much time is being dedicated, what that presence is costing you, and how you're measuring what you do. No need to fudge this, because you're the only one who needs to see it, and I won't tell on you.

How I'm Involved with Social Commerce So Far

- **Channels Used:** Do you have a personal Facebook account? Do you have a Business Page on Facebook? Are you a member of a group or chat board? Twitter? YouTube? Blog? You catch the drift, right? Just go ahead and list where your presence is. Create a second column and detail the number of fans, friends, or followers for each channel you're on.
- **Time Spent Weekly:** How much time are you spending weekly on social marketing? Do you actually have to spend this much time? If this is something performed by a resource or staff member, think about the time this person is allocating to related tasks. Is it a cost-effective use of time? What other tasks could be done instead? How much is your staff's time on social media costing your business?
- **Measures Used:** What tools or platforms do you use? How do you know you are being effective on social media? Do you have a way to track your activities to ensure you're meeting your goals and objectives? What do you gain from those fans, followers, retweets, views, comments, Likes, etc.? Do these things lead to increased click-through rates? (Don't stress too much if you don't have measures, because a lot of people don't. You'll learn a lot more about this in the chapters that follow.)
- **Competitor Profiles:** What? You don't know? You better freaking know! Go right now and search the social media channels

for your competitors. Take a look at *exactly* what they are doing. What is working? What is not? How will you jump in and work it, too? Get in there and do this step right now, 'cause ultimately your competition in the real world is your competitor on social media. But here's the bonus! If you went to visit a competitor's place of business in the real world, the important stuff—strategies, papers, phone numbers, etc.—would be hidden before you were shown around. No way would your competitors let you see them mixing the secret sauce. However, in social media, the sauce recipe is right there out in the *open* for you to see, analyze, and use to strategize with. Everything they have done is right there for you to see, so go get it!

Okay, now that you know what you have and haven't done, you can begin looking forward. Here's your chance to define your business objectives for using social media and decide what you want to accomplish. It's important to be as specific as you can be.

What I Want to Do from Now On

- **My Social Commerce Objectives:** Begin with the basics: number of followers, sales increase, videos on channel, brand management, customer acquisition, etc. Now explain exactly what these will do and how they will impact your business. It is okay to start with the thirty-thousand-foot view here, but as you move along, challenge yourself to get more and more detailed.
- **I Want to Begin with This Product:** Which products do you want to focus on? Who is using the product? Who is the customer? How do you segment and plan which product to talk about?
- **I Want to Influence This Part of the Sales Funnel:** Take a second and flip back to Chapter 4 and the sales funnel. How will your social media efforts affect awareness? Brand loyalty? Cross-selling? Customer service issues? Gathering UGC? Look at all of these areas and apply the ones most important to your success.
- **Next Year at This Time I Want to Be ... :** This is the one that is always my favorite, 'cause you really get to let your thought

process go bananas. I don't care how big or small you go, just go to where you feel comfortable! How many followers? YouTube views? Fans? Feedback rating? Whatever it is, just make sure you are going for just a twelve-month period. I don't think it is realistic to project more than one year out, especially in social media where things change and move rapidly. Of course this plan is a *living* plan, so feel free to adjust as necessary in the coming months once you put your plan into action and get a sense of how it's actually functioning as you implement it.

- **I Have My Eye on Trying These New Platforms and Tools:** Every day there is something new in social media marketing. There is a new tool, a new platform, or a new tactic. Is there some new channel that you want to implement? What new technology is available that you would like to use? How will it help your positioning in the market?

Well, you may be feeling exhausted by now, so I'll give you a little boost. Below you'll see a list of potential business objectives you can address through social media. I've even organized them by category, like a menu, so that you can easily select one from Column A and one from Column B. Or even more, of course.

Brand Awareness

Increase brand awareness.

Reach a specific audience.

Brand your staff as experts.

Get your customers to talk to one another.

Gather comments, feedback, photos, or video (UGC).

Get press coverage.

Understand what people are saying about your brand.

Customer Relations

Manage your reputation.

Get feedback.

Share information.

Build your e-mail list.

Provide insights about products.

Answer questions.

Share stories about our business, products, and services.

Promotion

Get press coverage.
Build excitement about an upcoming product.
Promote an event.
Get your customers talking (word-of-mouth ads, and they're free).
Get people to take action.

Networking

Stay informed with news about your products.
Keep informed about changes to your marketplace.
Build a community.
Connect with other like-minded businesspeople.

Sales

Generate leads.
Increase store traffic.
Improve sales.
Increase relevant visitor traffic and page rankings.

THE MORNING JOLT

So, you're done, right? You didn't skip over the last few pages and join me here unprepared, right? Okay, I'll take your word for it. As a reward for all the thinking you've just done, I'm going to let you look over my shoulder as I counsel our imaginary entrepreneur, Janice, through her planning and strategy session, so you can see how all of your thinking can be put into place and turned into action.

Janice owns a neighborhood coffee shop, the Morning Jolt. She and her partner have been in business for about ten years. They've weathered a lot through those years. Some of it has been helpful. People's increasing knowledge about good coffee and the availability of it in American culture during the last decade has been great. The arrival of a new Starbucks in her neighborhood and McDonald's selling great coffee has brought competition that Janice survived but simply never expected. How can Janice use social commerce and the Five Fingers to supercharge her small local coffee shop?

Janice gave the following answers as she assessed her current social commerce strategy:

Which social media channels are you currently using, Janice?

Channels Used: Currently I use both Facebook and Twitter, but only on a personal level to keep up with friends and family. We do not really have, nor have we thought much about, social for our business. I feel a little behind the times. I really want to get started with this wave, but it also has to pay off. I am very active daily in my business, and I can carve out time to work on my social commerce, but it has to pay off.

Time Spent Weekly: Right now I spend two or three hours a week in social, just browsing around and chatting with friends. We just opened a little store online where we sell Keurig coffeemakers and pods. They've been pretty popular in-store at the coffee shop. The locals come in regularly for the camaraderie and conversation or just to find a place to get away and work. Recently having a few items to sell has helped boost our bottom line slightly. So we just thought about putting up a web store. There has been very little activity there, but I did spend time uploading the coffeemakers and some of the coffee we sell for Keurig. If I got really serious about this, I could spend two to three hours a day on social commerce for sure.

Measures Used: I have not used any tool or platforms. This is an area that I know absolutely *nothing* about ... sorry.

You Can't Improve What You Don't Measure

Okay, I can't help myself. I have to step in here with this one. There are lots of great ways to measure your progress on social networks. Throughout the rest of this book, we'll look at ways to measure progress for each of the different platforms we study. But, for now, some measuring tools I think you'll find useful are the following:

1. SproutSocial.com: A powerful, yet affordable solution for small and medium businesses. It is a high-quality product with significant value for the user.
2. Viralheat.com: A platform to monitor "share of voice" with monitoring and management tools any business can afford.
3. SocialBro.com: Accurate information about your Twitter community. This site will help you determine who is influencing the community you build around your brand and company. For example, you'll learn what country your followers come from, what languages they speak, and what they do when they're on Twitter.

Competitor Profile: I went in and checked on the local competitors. The local coffee shop did have a Facebook page with more than sixteen hundred fans, and its webmaster was posting and chatting with customers. The webmaster even posted the story from the local newspaper about the store. When I looked at frequency of posting, though, it was slow; only eleven posts since October, so fewer than two per month. The local shop had a Twitter account, but it looked abandoned. The last tweet was in June of last year!

Now of course Starbucks was doing *big* things with fans and followers and content. Its Facebook page had 33 million followers for the national page, with postings three to five times a week on average. A lot of pictures were posted of the coffee and confections it sells. Starbucks has 3 million followers on Twitter and posts reminders for people to join up for its coffee club. It also has links to blog posts, and it was retweeting stories about Starbucks in the press. It was letting people know about drink specials in stores and advertising the availability of gift cards. But, as I explored, I also noticed there was no local page for the Starbucks shop located near us. Maybe that's an opportunity for me.

Now and Next Year, Too

My Social Commerce Objectives: I really want to get a Facebook page for the coffee shop and have a blog set up, too. I have 137 friends on Facebook now. Some are family and personal and others are people I have met from our business. We would use this page to make people aware of specials or events, and to establish the brand of the coffee shop.

I Want to Begin with This Product: I really want to begin with our coffeemakers as the first product. The customers could be anyone. We have all kinds of people buying from us. There are no real specific people, just all types.

I Want to Influence This Part of the Sales Funnel: When it comes to the parts of the funnel, I think the cross-selling and up-selling are important for us, and brand loyalty, too. People come in and compliment us on the service and the coffee. We need more people to see some of those comments from our customers.

Next Year at This Time I Want to Be ...: I would like to see five hundred followers of the Morning Jolt coffee shop on Facebook and Twitter. I want a blog set up and also the ability to sell some of our stuff on the web. I would like to see us making sure we get more comments from customers.

I Have My Eye on Trying These New Platforms and Tools: I just do not know where to begin or what I should be doing. One thing I do know is that I will not go another year without doing something! I guess it will be easiest to begin with Facebook. I just don't want to do it wrong and mess up.

JOHN TAKES JANICE BY THE HAND

We can give Janice some credit. She clearly took the time to answer the assessment questions and think about where she wants to be a year from now. She did pretty well in assessing where she is on social media now and what her competitors have been doing. Good for her. But, unfortunately, in looking forward, she fell short. She ended up not doing enough research, so she clearly has not learned all the lessons I was hoping you'd know by the time we got to this part of the book. Luckily, there are more chapters to go. Let's take a look at where Janice went wrong.

For the first half of the assessment, there really is no right or wrong answer. That exercise was meant to help Janice quantify what she has been doing and see where those efforts have left her. The same is true for you. You couldn't have made a mistake, because everything you've done so far has taught you something. It's the second half of the assessment—figuring out where to go next—where it's easy to slip back into pre-*Kick-Ass* days!

Not Enough Research

Janice began strong when I asked her to research her competitors. She came back with some pretty specific information about what they were doing with social media. But from thereon, she really fell off the mark. Maybe research isn't your thing, either, but you still have to do it. It's bad enough to postpone your research until you're sure you understand all the issues facing you, but it's another thing to not bother doing it at all.

I'm sure, faithful readers, you know that Janice really dropped the ball when she said "anybody" would buy her Keurig coffee machines, and she had customers from all over the spectrum.

That's probably true for her coffee shop customers, but it's crazy to think it's true for her potential online customers. In Chapter 2, we completed another exercise: creating a specific consumer to keep in mind when planning how to use social networks. Janice must have stepped out for a cup of coffee during this section of the book, because it took me less than five minutes to learn a lot about the people who may buy from Janice.

ICE MAKER

At Least Go Google It, for Crying Out Loud!

So who is Janice's customer? Well let's do a little research. This is a new venture so I have no customer data to look at. I need to begin at square one, so I am going to find that data to get me started by doing a Google search, simply by typing "who is the typical coffee drinker?" into its search engine. I quickly find the website for E-importz.com, a company that specializes in providing espresso business solutions to the specialty coffee industry. Janice should already know of this company's work. In a study published on its website in 2012, there is all of this great data about coffee drinkers:

Coffee is an 18 billion dollar market in the United States.

Coffee drinkers drink, on average, 3.1 cups a day.

50 percent of the U.S. population drinks some form of coffee (150 million daily drinkers).

The average espresso drive-through serves two- to three hundred cups a day.

The average price is $1.38 for a cup of regular coffee and $2.45 for espresso.

Men and women drink about the same amounts.

65 percent of coffee is drunk at breakfast and 30 percent between meals.

65 percent of coffee drinkers like it with sugar and/or cream, while 35 percent like it black.

Women drink it to relax. Men drink it to "get the job done."

Americans consume 400 million cups per day, making us number one in the world for coffee consumers.

Holy cow, one good Google search yielded me all that data, in just one click. I think we got a really great start for writing content! Now we know Americans love lots and lots of coffee. Janice could get even more specific and find out about the people who actually love coffee made by the machines she wants to sell.

If Janice had given it a bit more time, she may have decided to set up Google Alerts to check where people are gathering to talk about her product. I'll help her. To find these conversations I'll do some keyword searching. The two best tools for research-ing keywords are Google AdWords and Wordtracker. Both are free and easy to use.

While Janice is waiting for that data to come in, she could go back and search "Keurig customer reviews." Now she can see what people who have purchased the machines are saying about them. She can read through these to learn who they shop for, how they use it, and what they think about it.

The first site I visit shows a review written by a woman who bought a machine as a Christmas present for her adult son. She admits she's not a coffee drinker, but explains exactly why her son and her husband are. She goes on to explain why the Keurig was the right choice for her son, and she details her experience with the product, including how she fixed some issues that came up when the machine stopped working. In the end, she admits that even she loves the Keurig, because it makes her tea so quickly in the morning.

So now we know. This King Consumer bought the machine as a gift, suggesting it was a bit of a splurge. She's not going to be Janice's targeted King, but she is a customer. She had some trouble with the machine but was able to easily find help for addressing it. And, she is happy to have the device even though she only drinks tea. This is an awful lot of information to have gathered with just a few keystrokes, don't you think, Janice? It also shows a picture of a real customer who not only bought the product Janice sells but is also dramatically different from the type of customer Janice may have thought she had. That's a whole lot better than passing off this vital question with the lame response that she was selling it to "anyone!"

Missed Opportunities

Janice was able to pull things from the sales funnel to add to her objectives, but she failed to even try to say how she would achieve those objectives, and some of them are pretty easy. How hard is it to ask your most loyal customers, who you see all the time, to "Like" your Facebook page, post a review, make a positive comment, or share your blog post? There were plenty of opportunities to begin and, although her first task was to complete the assessment, she could have been applying what she already knew to plan how to achieve her objectives.

If I were sitting here with Janice right now, I'd give a pretty good review for answering the assessment, but I'd also push her to do more. As we continue with this book, you're going to learn about new platforms and techniques with each chapter. I need you to come along with me while also keeping in mind all the things you learned in Part One. You've already come half the way to social commerce finesse, so let's keep it up.

IT'S ALIVE, SO KEEP PAYING ATTENTION TO IT!

I expect you might be a bit exhausted, what with having just completed a detailed assessment of your business, your social commerce life so far, and your next twelve months full of goals and objectives. Then we did the same for Janice's business. I know it was no picnic. But now you have a plan, and as you move through your social commerce work, you'll be doing it with purpose. We've stepped into the nuts-and-bolts part of this book. You've spent many pages getting yourself ready for this, and now you are. You'll take this assessment along with your very specific and measurable business objectives, and move into the next twelve months ready to watch your business grow and your profits increase.

If you work alone, post your plan and objectives right next to your work space. Make them a part of what you do, think about, learn, plan for, and consider every day. If you have employees, or you hire freelance help, share your assessment and objectives with your staff. Let them give you their input and recommend some changes and suggestions you may not have thought about. You should have a whole new view of your operation based on what you've done in this chapter, and that view can only be enriched by having the input of the others who know your operation from the inside. Nothing here was set in cement, so you can always come back and recalibrate your efforts if you need to. As a matter of fact, that's exactly what you'll have to do in order to make progress and achieve your objectives. So, the gotcha in this chapter is that you'll continue on—and endlessly—studying and improving everything you do for your business. Now you have a step-by-step plan for doing that through social commerce.

SUMO LESSON

Janice had some tough lessons to learn. She was thinking toward social commerce, but she was still solidly stuck in the model of her brick-and-mortar store. This led her to make some simple but avoidable mistakes. She assumed who her King Consumer was based on the people who came into her store. The people who stop by the neighborhood coffee shop to pick up a cup on their way to work are not necessarily the same people who will visit her online store and buy her products there. She has to stop thinking of her shop customers as her only Kings.

She also has to stop putting herself in a box as someone who has no clue as what to do with social commerce. She may have been that when she first picked up this book, but we've all learned a lot since then. Go back and reread how she answered the question about exploring new platforms and technologies in the coming year.

Okay, I'll help you out. Here's what Janice said:

I just do not know where to begin or what I should be doing. One thing I do know is that I will not go another year without doing something! I guess it will be easiest to begin with Facebook. I just don't want to do it wrong and mess up.

Oh, no, she didn't say that, did she? If she takes this approach, next year will come and find her every bit as clueless as she is now! She's learned a lot, and she's learned how to learn more. Janice needs Google Alerts. Janice needs to research to find out more about who her King Consumers really are. She needs to remember that once she finds those Kings, she's going to listen to them before she tries to engage them. You get the idea. The only way she could mess up is if she sets about to "do something." So, let's turn the page and get to work on what I consider to be central to your social commerce efforts. Getting your blog right is a great place to begin.

That's a Rap!

✔ I know better than to just start posting stuff on social networks and call it a social commerce plan.

✔ I don't love self-assessment, but I'm going to do it anyway.

✔ I have to begin with where I am now, but I should put even more thought into how I want to proceed.

✔ I will not skip over the research part. Research lets me learn things my competitors don't want me to know.

✔ I can already begin framing my future objectives based on the sales funnel I learned about in Chapter 4.

✔ I can use some of the Five Fingers to begin planning my steps into social commerce.

✔ I will take with me all the things I've already learned as we move forward.

CHAPTER 7

WordPress:
Spread Your Seeds

"Big fields await the wide awake man."

—Elijah Muhammad

B ack in Chapter 3, I told you about the day I was hanging out in the backyard pool, just watching the bees buzzing around in my I-need-a-good-mow lawn. You may remember I found the activity inspirational when I realized that although most folks saw "pollinating," I saw "nectar gathering." This was a good insight, and I'm happy to say that it wasn't the only one I took from that pleasant afternoon. You see, when you let your lawn get overgrown, it can lead to more than one life lesson. This one came in the form of a patch of dandelions.

Every last one of those dandelion seeds comes complete with its own tiny parachute. Once the seeds have matured and are ready to spread, either the wind or a random child (or fun-loving adult!) will come along and scatter those parachutes on a breeze. Most of them won't go too far. Unless it's a pretty windy day or a pretty determined kid, those seeds will settle somewhere in the same neighborhood where the mama dandelion did. But a few of those parachutes will get caught on a gust. They'll rise up and travel farther away from the parent plant than the other seeds will go, which will give them a whole different environment to populate and save them from having to compete with all the other dandelions for the limited resources of my now-dandelion-filled backyard. If you're reading this and you're a landscaper, hit me up. My yard sucks!

You're going to use your blog as the dandelion at the center of your social commerce plan. It, and all the other content you create, will take your brand, your reputation, and your business into new and far-flung fields where there will be plenty of opportunity to spread out and tap new resources. Your blog is going to be the hub of the wheel that drives your social commerce efforts, just like the big head of white fuzz is the center that begins the lives of all those soon-to-be dandelions. A blog gives you freedom to create, explore, and bring your own business brand and personality to life as you engage your King Consumers. You don't have to be a great writer. The only thing you have to be is knowledgeable about your business, your products, your customers, and their needs.

I won't argue with you, blogging *is* old school. But even as one of the earliest social media tools we have, its power still can't be denied. Yes, back in the dark days—before everything began floating around on the Cloud—people used online services, such as AOL, to gather digitally. The forums on those services were early social media platforms, and the communities were strong and robust, even if minuscule by today's standards. But when it comes to controlling the content of your brand and business, and spreading that content according to your own plans and needs, nothing gives you more bang for the buck than a blog. You're going to connect your blog and link it all over social media, with a strategic plan of course. You'll find your blog will be great for helping you energize the Fifth Finger, Brand Awareness, and it will also broaden your sales funnel, the First Finger. But before you can put these fingers to work, you have to get your systems in place and create some content. Don't panic, because I'm here to help.

First let's do a little reality check. How many of you out there can swim? How many of you out there enjoy swimming as great exercise? How many of you once swam on a competitive team at school or in your community? Now, how many of you can compete with Michael Phelps, winner of twenty-two Olympic medals? Yeah, that's what I thought. It's easy to psych yourself out when it comes to starting a blog. It seems big. It seems you have to get it right. It seems like a lot of work when you'd rather be paying attention to other parts of your business. Trust me when I tell you that you can easily have a blog up and running in a single afternoon, and I'm not saying this just because I wrote this book. I'm saying it because it's really not that hard, and I know how to help. Think about it. The last time you were hanging out on the beach watching your kids splash in the surf, it never occurred to you to wonder if the lifeguards could beat Michael Phelps in a race. But if you've ever seen those lifeguards jump into action to help someone in the water, then you know, with no second thoughts, they can swim just fine. You can showcase your business in a blog just fine, too.

OKAY, SO WHY WORDPRESS?

Wait a minute. I hear some protests in the back: "John, I already have a blog someplace else." Good for you, and I mean that. And you, over there, shut your trap. I don't own the stock, wise guy. You can have blogs all over the web, but that's not going to get you out of having a WordPress one, too. WordPress is a blogging tool, sure, but it's so much more than that. It's a content management system (CMS), and that's why you need to be using it.

The CMS functions that WordPress offers give you a single dashboard that allows you to create, organize, publish, distribute, and engage your Kings all from one single platform. Now some of you may be thinking, "So does YouTube or Facebook." Yes, they do. However when you add WordPress to your plan, you get a system that will "talk" to and engage not only Facebook and YouTube, but also Twitter, Pinterest, Google+, LinkedIn, Instagram, and dozens of other sites at the same time (see Figure 7-1). Now this is what WordPress can do as a content management system.

With WordPress, you'll be able to host and launch not only your words but also your photos, videos, slide shows, audio files, and everything else you want to share. WordPress makes it very simple with an overwhelming number of plug-ins—more than 25,700 the last time I checked—created by other members of the WordPress community and available for everyone to share. Plug-ins are software adaptations that add functionality to your blog you'd otherwise need impressive software skills to do yourself.

That's another great thing about WordPress. It's an open source tool, which means two things. One is that software

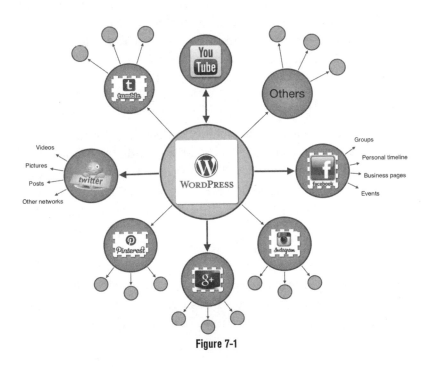

Figure 7-1

developers are free to make changes, which, of course, doesn't have anything to do with us. More importantly, the open source nature of WordPress means you are free to use it without charge for whatever you want to accomplish with your blog. It's pretty tough to beat free.

ICE MAKER

Use WordPress.org

There are two versions of WordPress:WordPress.com and Word-Press.org. WordPress.com is the free hosted version, which means WordPress gives you space on its servers to host your blog. That's not the one I want you to use. I'll explain more later, but for now just do what I say and download WordPress.org.

You Mean Free? As In, It Won't Cost Me Anything?

Well, no, not exactly. Although you'll be able to use WordPress for free, and that's huge, you'll still need to register with a host site to get a domain name and space on the host's servers for your blog and other content. There are many such host sites, but I like these two: HostGator and Bluehost. You won't need the most expensive option, but even those options are reasonable. You can expect to pay from about $5 to $15 per month. The difference in the prices reflect options, such as toll-free customer support. Once you sign up, the software for the host will simply download and install with a single click.

It Is Simple to Begin

You'll be happy to know that getting your WordPress blog up and running is as simple as clicking your mouse and keyboarding. Plus, you'll find that WordPress offers almost endless customization options. I'm not going to try to make you an expert in creating and maintaining an amazing WordPress blog. You do not need to be the Michael Phelps of the blog world. I'm not even going to walk you through the process. It's so simple that you already have all the experience and technological savvy you're going to need to do that. If you need more guidance, you can find it on the WordPress site, or you search on YouTube for some great tutorials that will actually walk you through the process. But, trust me, the best thing to do is just get on the site and start playing around with it. You'll see how easy the whole thing is. Instead, I'm going to help you set up your blog with the most useful tools I know, and that means plug-ins.

⬇ ICE MAKER

WordPress Plug-ins You Should Have Right Now

When you go to the WordPress directory of plug-ins, it's easy to get overwhelmed with the volume of choices. With so many to choose from, and all for free, it's tempting to try a bunch.

Here are just a few of my favorites.

1. All in One SEO Pack: Automatically optimize your blog for search engines. You probably remember that Google, for example, loves blogs, and this plug-in will help ensure that yours gets its rightful place in the results. Best of all, you only have to install it and let it run. If you're just beginning with SEO, you won't even have to make decisions right now. Just let it do its thing. This one little plug-in will help you achieve your Fourth-Finger goals, don't you think?

2. Google Analytics: This one adds the Java script you'll need to use with your blog. It enables Google Analytics to run the script on every blog page. You'll need to create an account (http://www.google.com/analytics/), but you should have one of these anyway.

3. Google Author Link: Use this to store your Google+ URL and then each page and post of your blog will have the required link in the HTML head. Did I go too far? Okay,

in other words, it will allow you to automatically link your Google+ profile to your blog and vice versa.

4. Shareaholic: Here's a very cool plug-in that adds an eye-catching social bookmarking menu to your blog. Now, as your Kings read your content, they only have to click one button to share it with their social networks. Clicking only one button will make it easy for them to spread those seeds you'll be launching!

OKAY, BUT WHAT SHOULD I WRITE?

When we decide to add social marketing to our businesses we need that to mean something. As you know, I am not really interested in making friends really, nor am I interested in having followers. No, I am *most* interested in making money. My goal with my blog—as yours should also be—is to get the King Consumer to buy. We want those who do already buy to buy more frequently, more consistently, and with bigger cart values on each shopping trip.

So others may talk to you about blogging and keywords and relevancy for SEO and blah, blah, blah ... I want to talk about showing you the money! That is what we are here for and that is the difference between social marketing and social commerce, right? Cool, baby!

You should have an idea of what types of information your Kings are searching for, now that you've been busy listening to them and paying attention to what they're saying all over the web. You probably also have a list of ideas you gathered from your Google Alerts that you set up from Chapter 4. You did set them up, right? Of course, I thought so. So now I'm going to make it easy by giving you some guidance about where you can begin. Then I'll share a few examples of how I've used my blog with good results. Again, we're not interested in winning any blogging awards, so don't be intimidated by that blank page staring at you.

⬇ ICE MAKER

You've Got Frequently Asked Questions, Right?

I challenge you to go take a look at your most frequently asked questions (FAQs). I'm talking about the range of things that you customers have been asking you, whether that's about your products, your policies, or your services. Take the top questions—ten if you have them, but five will do, too—and polish them up in complete answers. Boom! You've got your first blog entry. Done and done! No more blank page.

How Often Should I Write?

When people ask me how often they should write for their blog, I always say consistency and quality matter more than frequency. So, let's look at this. If what you can produce is one blog posting a week, but it's a good one and you can keep blogging every single week, then that's what you should do. If you can and want to do more, that's fine, as long as you can sustain it. You will ultimately "train" the people who follow your blog to expect a new posting as often as you provide one. Just be sure that what you write is very relevant to your audience. That is far more important that the frequency.

I usually sit down once a month and create all the content I plan to use in the month ahead. My thought is that I like to do fifteen to twenty-five postings a month. In between my written blog posts, I like to sprinkle in some other things I find and think I'd like to share, such as videos, photos, links, and other content. You can even let some of your staff write postings, if they are inclined and able. Just be sure to create a system you can sustain, and you'll be fine.

If You Need Help, Admit It

I had hoped my first blog would generate more traffic for my website. This was my objective when I decided to start writing. I wrote a few dozen posts and sat back to wait and see what would happen. There was only so much I could think up that would be interesting to the King Consumers who came to look at my products, a mix of hip-hop jewelry, hats, shoelaces, and flags. Well, with a couple dozen posts under my belt, I noticed very little traffic coming from the blog and almost none coming from the blog to my web store. Clearly, something wasn't working the way I'd expected it would.

But, like you, I had a clear idea of who my Kings were. They were young, ranging in age from fifteen to twenty-nine. They liked hip-hop music and were into basketball. They also loved everything to do with celebrities in the music world, sports, and Hollywood. Perez Hilton's gossipy website was blowing up, and his celebrity gossip blog was getting lots of press. He was turning into a really big deal. That got me thinking about my own Kings. They love celebrity gossip! This revelation was frustrating, because now I wanted a celebrity gossip site geared toward an urban hip-hop crowd that was way outside my own demographic group. I was not up to speed on what or even who was trendy in that particular audience.

So I put an ad on Craigslist for a blog writer. I said this person had to love urban hip-hop and know who was hot in music and sports. I ended up hiring a twenty-four-year-old who showed she could provide the skills we needed. I paid her $50 a week. Her job was simply to write celebrity gossip stories of about three- to five hundred words, five to seven times a week. I did not give a crap about keywords or putting my jewelry in the blog posts or anything like that. All I wanted was content that was relevant to my audience of possible King Consumers. This was the *top* of the sales funnel! She was great at it. In the second week, her stories were already generating ten times the traffic my dumb, boring posts were. I clearly was not the right man for this particular job.

"Sell" Yourself Some Ad Space!

Now, everyone who has a popular blog—celebrity gossip or not—makes money selling ad space on their sites. You know those ads are just all over the place, and no one who uses the Internet expects anything different. The space is valuable real estate. I had a dilemma when it came to online advertising for my business at the time. My product mix just could not support the cost of paid online ads. I sold items costing less than $10, and many cost less than $5. Even at $0.05 a click on Google AdWords, it was too expensive to get enough customers to justify spending the money. Of course, my blog was the answer.

Once my new celebrity blog began generating traffic, I simply put my own ads into those spaces on my blog where everyone expects to see ads. Yep, you get the picture? All the banner ads were ours. All the underlined links went to our company, and all the ads top and bottom on the blog posts were for us, too. So the blog was not at all about our business or products, but we created blog *content* to function as bait to get consumers in our target demographic to read it and see our ads. And by getting the relevant content to our chosen King Consumers we got lots and lots of traffic. This is content in context, and you already know that means money.

It was much cheaper to pay our freelance writer $250 a month to make content we could use to place our ads for lead generation than it would have been to buy ads on someone else's site. This technique was freaking brilliant! I was floored with how well it worked. The conversion rate of this blog was higher than anything we ever got with paid ads. And it really cost us a fraction of a penny to get leads. In just six weeks, the blog was getting more than eleven thousand hits a month. Of that crowd, 9 percent were clicking on the ads, and of that group 11 to 12 percent became new buyers. That's *money*!

So if you do that math—and trust me, I did—11,000 readers brought in 990 clicks and 109 of those people clicking made a purchase. Our average cart size was $14 at the time, so that was generating $1,526 from basically $250 worth of paid blog posts. The cool thing was that every week the traffic was getting better!

We moved along happy and healthy for about four months. That's just about the time I learned the lesson I shared with you earlier about WordPress.org versus WordPress.com. Suddenly, I got a call from my blog writer that she couldn't log into our blog. When I went to investigate, I learned all of our activity on our blog had actually violated the terms by which I could use WordPress.com. I tell you this, just so you know, so many of my lessons were learned this hard way, and not just by hanging out in the backyard pool!

Bet You Can't Stop at Just One

Once you start to see the kind of results that are possible through your blog, I'm willing to bet you won't be able to stop at just one. I know I couldn't. Once I started selling black hair products, we created a blog about black hair and fashion. When I sold athletic gear, we started a sports fan blog. Blogs gave us a way to have multiple streams of traffic coming to us from content that was so simple to write, I could have hired a clever high school student to do it. Wait a minute … I did hire clever high school students for some of these projects. We're only blogging for dollars, and the more relevant content I can scatter from my dandelion puff, the more seeds of commerce I can plant all over the world of social media. That's what makes all this social commerce, baby! It's all about the money.

SUMO LESSON

Because I had already discovered so much success from using my blog to generate traffic and sales, I was ready when a great opportunity came along during the Super Bowl of 2012. My mind is always thinking about finding the right context for the content my Kings will want. It's habit now. When I saw Madonna fall during her performance at the half-time show that year, I knew I was golden. I was recording the Super Bowl, and so I captured that fall. I posted it on a blog, and it got over three thousand hits in just two hours! This little slip got me the best traffic I've ever had from any blog posting. The recording itself was not that important, but it generated a lot of traffic, and some of that traffic came to our website to shop. So, that is a simple and clear look at how you can snare your Kings by placing *their* high-interest content in the right context for them to enjoy so they will then take action by shopping with you.

That's a Rap!

- ✓ I will use my WordPress blog as the center of everything else I do in social commerce.
- ✓ I have signed up for a WordPress.org blog and not a WordPress.com one.
- ✓ I have downloaded John's recommended WordPress plug-ins.
- ✓ I have a blog post ready to go, because I've answered my most frequently asked questions.
- ✓ I've begun thinking about the content my Kings will want and how I can craft the right context to place it in.
- ✓ I know I don't have to spend money on ads, as long as I have my WordPress blog.

CHAPTER 8

Facebook Turns Me On!

"I don't promote boxing. I promote people. Boxing is
a catalyst to bring people together."

—Don King

Okay, so now that you've got your WordPress blog up
and running, it's time to show you how to use your
content, and the content your King Consumers will generate, to
spread your dandelion seeds all over the web. You already know,
I'm not going to mess around with who has the most Likes or
the greatest number of comments. If it doesn't generate income,
neither one of us has time for it. Facebook stands alone in the
social commerce world for a good number of reasons we'll be
exploring. But in a sense, Facebook itself is not a new concept.

In my opinion, Facebook is just a glorified update to that old
site of the 1990s, America Online (AOL). It is very similar to what
AOL was in the past, because Facebook is a walled community
where people have gathered for the purpose of communicating,
sharing insights, information, and friendship. We could even call
Facebook an AOL 2.0 and be close to the truth. Whatever you
personally might think about Facebook itself, you must embrace
its importance in our social commerce strategy and learn to har-
ness its incredible power. Facebook can boast more than 1 billion
people served, and every last one of them decided to willingly join
the site's closed community. It only stands to reason that you're

very likely to find a good many of your current customers there, and *their* networks all represent potential future King Consumers just waiting to discover what you're doing with their "friends."

We're going to pull Facebook out of the general social commerce mix to use very specifically, but at the same time, many of the techniques and tips you'll learn about here can be applied on other sites to promote your social commerce efforts. I want you to keep that tucked away in the back of your mind while we move forward. Treating Facebook as a separate entity makes sense when you consider what the site can do. It's now way more than a social network.

Facebook is a *platform*, a tool so powerful that companies use it as a business starter. Consider Zynga. You haven't heard of that company? Well, maybe not, but the folks at Zynga launched a little game on Facebook called FarmVille. Oh, okay, now I've got your attention. The people behind Zynga used gaming on the Facebook platform to occupy the minds of millions of people with a silly farming game! Or look at Pinterest. It would not even be on people's lips if the folks at Pinterest did not integrate their social sharing tool with Facebook from the start. You get my point. Facebook is an ecosystem that cannot be ignored. We'll use this huge ecosystem to create and manage your very own small ecosystems—populated by your proven customers and their as-yet-untapped Facebook networks. And those smaller ecosystems? Well, they'll be completely controlled by *you*. So let's get to it.

FACEBOOK'S PLACE IN YOUR SOCIAL COMMERCE PLAN

Let's start by taking a look at Facebook's role in your social commerce plan. It has a special place in the dandelion puff you plan to use to spread your brand and your business. As you'll see, it has quite a lot of power to keep your newly planted seedlings growing among, maybe, the most important group of King Consumers you know: your current customers. You'll also find that Facebook's power will allow you to tap more than one of our Five Fingers (see Chapter 4). We've definitely got the sales funnel covered here and wait till you see what you can do with customer relationship management (CRM) and user generated content (UGC)! We've just begun to spread those dandelion seeds, and already the potential opportunities can make you dizzy. Let's first look at the anemic way most businesses now use Facebook.

I'll take a guess: You have a Facebook page for your business. You asked your Facebook friends to Like your page, and they have. From time to time you post something there about a new product or promotion. But there's probably not a lot happening there for you. If you decide to do nothing but push, push, push, and send out one marketing message after another, you can hang it up right now. Your followers will tune you out and completely ignore you. Oh, your actual friends may be too polite to tell you that you're a total pain in the ass, but they're still not going to pay any attention to you. You really don't need them to actually like you. You just need them to like what you sell at the price you sell it for.

The IBM Institute for Business Value released a study at the end of 2012 that demonstrates an interesting disconnect between what companies think people want from them on social media and what people actually do want. The results were more than a little shocking, as you see in Figure 8-1. IBM learned businesses use social media to reach their customers because they believe those customers want to "learn about the products" (73 percent) and gather "general information" (71 percent). When IBM asked the same question of *consumers*, the findings show exactly how wrong most businesspeople are about the subject. The top two answers from the consumers—who had actually decided to go to

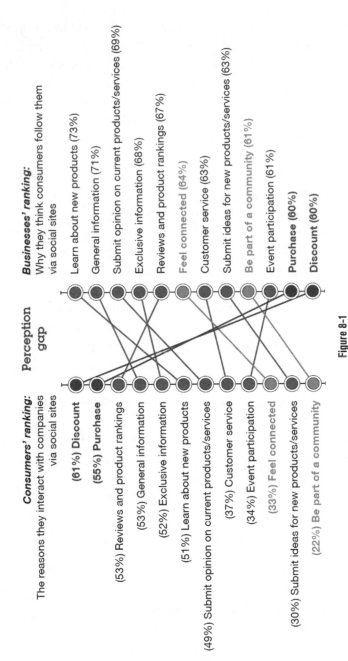

Figure 8-1

Courtesy of International Business Machines Corporation, © 2013 International Business Machines Corporation.

social media sites, so they know why they did—were "discounts" (61 percent) and "purchases" (55 percent).

The Power to Share Whatever They Want and Be Connected

According to our friend Mark Zuckerberg, that's why he first wanted to create Facebook: "Our mission is to make the world more open and connected. We do this by giving people the power to share whatever they want and be connected to whoever they want, no matter where they are." Okay, let's take a moment to just let that sink in here: the power to share what you want, when you want, and wherever you are. That makes the clay that is Facebook completely malleable. You can shape it and form it to fit any business model at all, and I do mean *any*. This sort of power comes with a lot of responsibility, and I'm here to make sure you use the power responsibly. If the best you've come up with so far is a Facebook strategy consisting of pressing the Facebook button on all your product pages and blasting your wall and your friends' walls with all the crap you sell, *stop* it now! You are abusing the power by using a truly powerful system so poorly. You can do better.

A Home for Your King Consumers

Facebook is a place for your existing customers to interact with you and with one another. The site is perfect for inviting your Kings into your parlor, sharing special treats with them, and making them feel royally connected to you and all that you have to offer them as they bask in the appreciation you so clearly have for them. Focus on treating your Kings royally, and you'll not only get them to stick around and shop, but you'll also push them deeper into the sales funnel (see Chapter 4), making your business their go-to destination whenever they want whatever you sell. As if that's not enough, you'll also craft a public window on Facebook through which everyone who does *not* belong to your

Kings' networks can see. Now they'll know there's something special going on around your Facebook presence. You'll get to keep your existing customers happy and satisfied. At the same time, you'll entice new customers with glimpses of what can be possible if they join the elite group of people who currently shop with you. Intrigued? Good, I thought you might be!

EVER-CHANGING CONTENT FOR THE EVER-CHANGING FACE OF FACEBOOK

What would you say is the best part Facebook? Okay, I'll tell you. It's not stagnant. It doesn't stay the same. The results change all the time and everything fluctuates. What's the biggest problem with Facebook? Okay, I'll tell you again. It's not stagnant. It doesn't stay the same. It changes all the time. If you are to succeed on Facebook, you're going to have to let the research you've done on your King Consumers and the listening you've been doing to their conversations and postings guide you to posting frequently and intelligently on Facebook and delve deeper into the interests your King Consumers have shared.

Facebook interaction is brisk. Don't like what is in your thread on Facebook? Wait thirty seconds! It will change. So the frequency of a platform like Facebook is going to be different from the frequency of your blog posts. I think you should use Facebook daily. If that's not possible, then post three to five times weekly at the very least. Also be sure to take into account that Facebook is very visual and mobile, and big picture thoughts, graphs, charts, and photography are all the rage. Keep what you post simple and shareable. A good Facebook strategy for content production is a mix of visual content and videos. Keep it 80 percent fun, but also make sure there are some calls to take action, because you want to bring those prospective consumers and your proven purchasers closer to and deeper into the sales funnel.

⬇ ICE MAKER

The Pace Is Fast, So Keep It Coming

Posts to Facebook business pages get stale fast, and the nature of Facebook users is that they need to see regular activity to stay engaged. That's why you see people checking Facebook throughout the day with their smartphones! Remember, we do *not* need to make up all our own posts. We can easily find great and relevant subject matter from other posters on Facebook and repost or "Share" it on our own walls. It actually helps to cement your place in the community when you share what your network is talking about. So use both original and reposted stuff. Just keep it coming.

The Many Faces You Can Have on Facebook

You can think two dimensionally about your blog. You find it, create it, post it, and then do it again. But you're going to have to think multidimensionally about Facebook if you want to drill down to really meaningful interactions with your King Consumers.

Let's say, for example, that you sell pet supplies. You have a Facebook page for your general business where you post all types of information and links. You may follow the Humane Society of the United States. You may follow your local animal shelter. Your page is alive with general information about the health and well-being of your customers' pets. Consider, in addition to this page, having a separate page for your cat lovers and one for your dog lovers. You can have as many Facebook pages as you want, so let's say you put one up to serve bird owners, another one for small "pocket" pets, one for ferrets, and another for reptiles and aquarium pets. Did somebody say content in context? Yeah, I think we've got it!

Now you have pages to attract every kind of pet owner you sell products to. The interaction on your micro-niche Facebook page for reptiles will be so specific, you can really charm those snake lovers with exactly the information they need. You'll also be privy to far more intense and detailed conversations and interactions about the subject of owning reptiles. That will help you zero in on what reptile owners are concerned about and what they need to properly take care of their pets. You can see the potential in this type of fragmented customer interaction, I'm sure. You're still dealing with all the potential pet owners in the entire world, but you've made a cozy spot under a heat lamp for the reptile owners who have shopped or will shop with you. That's a place they'll return to, and frequently, not only because you post interesting things there, but because they've found the community you've grown that includes lots of other people who love living with snakes. I absolutely did this with my bandana-folding videos; I created separate bandana sites and Facebook pages specifically for folding bandanas.

All your products represent areas you can market. The coolest thing about this is that when you get it right, the community will take over. Ultimately you can push people from your main community into your smaller-community pages and vice versa. It's hard to get people interested in your business pages, but if you create groups and pages relevant to very specific parts of your inventory, people will go there to gather and converse. And you can become very engaged with your current customer base in these smaller ecosystems you've created, making it that much easier to get them to pay attention to your Facebook page. The more they engage with you and you engage with them, the more their friends and followers will see what you're doing. Your customers then become essential cheerleaders for your business.

So, don't look at Facebook in such a linear fashion. I hear it all the time: "Oh, we have to go get people to Like our page, and if they Like us, then some of those people will buy from us." Yeah, that's true, but that produces a very low rate of return. The real rate of return involves getting your current customers engaged with you in these small ecosystems (groups/pages/events) you've created. Here they can engage not only with you but also with each other—and then you've got it made. You control the ecosystems. You can see exactly who is engaged with you and how they are engaging. Now you can direct your marketing at your actual customers so discreetly and specifically, that they'll return to your Facebook ecosystem not only when they need another commodity, but also because you've allowed them to join a vibrant online community just as devoted to and crazy about their pets as your King Consumers are.

ICE MAKER

Facebook Gives. You Take Away.

Once you have your ecosystems in place, you can use Facebook Insights to see the analytics that represent your Kings. We'll take a look at this and other tools in a bit, but in the meantime, be aware that Facebook can be a source of huge amounts of information about your Kings, such as demographics about the average age of your Kings and what parts of the country they're from. You can see who is engaged with you. They only see this cool Facebook presence you've created, but you're using their visits to learn more about your business and your customers with each passing week.

General Content Strategies

So let's begin by giving your customers what they want. We need to make sure your strategy is completely focused on commerce, not media. In view of all this posting you're going to do, we don't want to lose track of why we've all gathered here, and that's to make money. So, sure, repost and let your ecosystems go wild, but be sure you still control that ecosystem by calling on your King Consumers to do specific things. They'll feel rewarded, but even better, so will you.

The 80/20 Rule definitely applies to your Facebook content. Your content should be split between 80 percent fun stuff, light information, and interaction and 20 percent direct calls to action or sales. If you mix it up like this, people will interact with you for both the fun and excitement, and they will buy for the thrills. Trust me. If, for every ten posts you make, one or two of them is a direct call to action, your Kings will engage directly with you.

There is an old adage that says "you have not because you ask not." The reason most folks never sell anything via Facebook is simply because they *never* ask. Of course you won't be overbearing about it—80 percent of the time you're mixing it up with fun and interesting stuff—but your Kings are here on your Facebook pages interacting with you. They know you sell things, so you don't have to pretend you don't. Offer your loyal followers discounts and specials. Be sure to give them what they crave regularly. Like Don Corleone said in *The Godfather*, "Make them an offer they can't refuse."

This means you stop making offers to your customers for general stuff like the chance to win an iPad for Liking your page. That's a lot of money to spend, and the truth is we don't really get customers engaged that way. It's much better to give your customers—who have already proven their interest in your business by sharing your Facebook presence—discounts on the products you sell. Now you get to offer, say, a 5 percent discount on their next order for Liking your page on Facebook. *Bang!* There they go, deeper into that sales funnel for up-selling and cross-selling. That call to action gets them to Like you, sure, but even better, it gets them to come back again and spend their money, along with their discount, of course. As my sister, Ro, likes to say, "Deuces!" We just accomplished two goals in one: We gave the customers what they wanted and they in turn did the same for us. Win-win! *Ka-ching, ka-ching!*

⚓ BREAKING **THE ICE**

Facebook Ads: Money Well Spent

Facebook offers users paid advertising. This is another area we could potentially spend a lot of time exploring. We could spend an entire book on paid advertising and pay-per-click (PPC) ads. Actually I am sure there are already several entire books on this subject. Pay-per-click advertising requires some in-depth understanding about how to track and measure the performance and analytics of the ads you're placing. If you're eager to give them a try, the Facebook platform allows you to dabble in PPC with a very user friendly interface.

Facebook ads are effective when you want to get laser-targeted visitors to your pages. They allow you to break down the advertising to reach specific demographics, and Facebook makes this feature very easy to use—maybe too easy. The money you'll spend is still the same whether they work or not. You will have to spend money to get eyeballs. But, if you really want to try PPC advertising, the Facebook ads system is a good place to do that. Just don't be surprised when you get the bill.

Business Versus Personal

People often ask me what they should put on their business profile versus what their personal Facebook profile. Here is my general rule: You should keep your business profiles business and keep your personal profiles *real*. What I mean is that your business allows you to chat with your customers, but just make sure you keep it in the business lane. You need not tell them what you are eating for lunch or that you've got to drop the kids off at soccer practice. Save that for the personal profile. Keep them engaged with you and your staff as the "people who work here and are eager to help you."

On your personal page, you can post all of those things your customers don't necessarily need to see, and you can still keep it real when it comes to your business, which is a very important part of your life, so you need not totally avoid a mention of it here or there. But do not get carried away with your marketing stuff on your personal page or people will begin to tune you out. Keep it personal. Keep it real. You will do just fine. And if you have an out-of-this-world sale going on, it won't hurt to mention it to your online buddies every once in a blue moon.

I like to keep my followers updated about which city I might be in like, "Hey, I am speaking in Cleveland this weekend. Hit me up if you want to do coffee or a drink." That would be me, looking to network or hang out with friends or followers while in a city. Now someone may ask where I am speaking, and then I will say come to this so-and-so conference. But I would not begin the conversation with, "Hey, register to hear me speak at the Cleveland Convention Center show and blah, blah, blah ... " You can see that's just too much obvious marketing.

Do That, But Please, Don't Do This

As you already well know, there are things you can do on social media that can't be undone. You're well-educated enough to know not to do the more boneheaded things you may have seen other people doing. For example, I really don't need to tell you that you will never, ever, not ever, and I mean never, engage in a public dispute on Facebook with a specific King Consumer who is proving to be a royal pain. But there are a whole lot of other, much less boneheaded, things you could innocently do, thinking they represent good strategy, when really, they are against Facebook rules. I'm here to save you from yourself. To stay current on the ever-evolving changes to Facebook policy, be sure to bookmark the Facebook Pages Guideline page at: http://www.facebook.com/page_guidelines.php

You want to use your Facebook business page to offer your loyal customers special Facebook-only deals or offers. This is a great way to get current fans to share your page, because people love to share special deals and offers with their friends—remember how dependent these Kings are on the recommendations of their friends. If you want to add an extra level of interaction, tie it into your status updates. For example, "Come enjoy our tax-free weekend from July 25–27. Keep an eye on our Fan Page for updates and the special code word you will need to take advantage." It's a basic example, but you get the idea. Invite your fans to take an action or to keep coming back to your fan page in exchange for a deal. Either way, keep them in the loop about ways to save, ways to use the products they are purchasing, and ways to share the good news about you with all of their friends. The more you "love them" the more they will love you back and spread that love. In addition to all the love you are giving your current customers, visitors to your Facebook page are seeing the cool-ass community they are *not* yet a part of. Oh my, the psychology of that ...

⬇ ICE MAKER

They Visit and Interact, Because They Like What You Do

My friend Melanie Maybe (you'll learn a lot more about her soon) operates an e-commerce business specializing in alternative fashions and accessories. She created such a cool Facebook page that her King Consumers routinely check in just to see what she's saying or doing in fashion these days. Melanie is now a fashion tastemaker. (Figure 8-2 shows a glimpse of her taste and Facebook image.) That's the kind of rapport you want to build with your Kings, too. Once they keep checking in with you because they like the destination you've made for them on Facebook, you can do all kinds of interesting things with them.

"Almost from the start the Facebook page was a success," Melanie told me. "Customers absolutely loved having the ability to see new stock, vote on things, give input, and get a response from us." Today, Melanie and her staff still interact routinely on the Tragic Beautiful Facebook page. Recent questions from her Kings include requests for specific brands of boots and a request for advice about matching a new hair-dye color with hair already dyed bluish black.

Now that her Kings consider Melanie a go-to resource for alternative fashion, they post questions to her Facebook page, asking if it's possible to buy specific products from her site. That's the kind of engagement with your Kings you hope to achieve, too.

Figure 8-2

Oh, and by the way, Melanie recommended the hot pink or bright-red hair dye. Then she posted pictures of each color to answer her King's question visually.

THE ROYAL TREATMENT FOR YOUR KING CONSUMERS

Every person on this earth wants to be treated like a VIP. I remember the last time I was in Las Vegas for a conference. The conference organizers rented a section of a club for an event. At the beginning of the event there were two lines: one for the VIPs and one for the regulars. Being a VIP is something everyone on that regular line wished to be. Even those who don't care about stature still want the hassle-free (no waiting in line) access that VIPs enjoy.

Take this into account when you're posting to your public-facing Facebook pages. Your King Consumers actually are your

VIPs, and Facebook is the place to treat them royally. Everyone else who views your Facebook pages or your Kings' Facebook pages gets to see the VIP treatment your current fans and customers are getting, but onlookers are not yet sharing in.

For example, suppose you sell shoes. You make a VIP list of customers who have already bought your shoes and you send those VIPs an e-mail, giving them first access to your new inventory before it hits the public site. You post about this on your general business Facebook page and invite your fans to join the VIP ranks. Now you've created an advantage for your VIPs and also shown this advantage, as well as your call to action, to your yet-to-be VIPs. These yet-to-be VIPs can't actually have your reward of early access to inventory until they take an action and sign up for "insider" treatment.

Now you are doing a lot more than just engaging on Facebook, because now you've got permission to directly market to your VIPs and all the other fans who will become VIPs. Of course, these are going to be your best King Consumers and your happiest cheerleaders. I can hear the conversation on Facebook now ... "Girl, you need to join the Shoe Market VIP list! They give us discounts and private inventory sales. Go Like their page!" ... *Deuces!*

Everyone wants to walk the VIP red carpet. So, once you get customers in VIP status, treat them as such. It goes a long way. Look to the travel industry for masterful treatment of the VIP. I do a lot of traveling. I am a Gold Medallion member with Delta, and I am treated like it. Delta gives me complimentary upgrades to First Class, checked bags with no fee, and first-boarding on all flights. Delta even puts tags on my luggage so they will come off the carousel before those of the "common" fliers. Look at that list, and you tell me how much money you think all this special treatment costs Delta. That's my point exactly. Delta treats me right, and in turn I am loyal to Delta. I keep flying with this airline so I can stay with its VIP status. And it costs the airline nothing, or next to nothing. Sure, I'm a Delta VIP, but that First Class seat was empty, or I wouldn't have gotten it. Even better than my loyalty to Delta is that it actually got props in my book! Here I am writing about how great being a Delta Skymiles member is, and it is costing Delta nothing! Zero! I am giving them totally free advertising, and why? Because this method works for Delta, and it will work for you, too.

Facebook Groups

One of the best things about Facebook is the ability to create a community, or multiple communities, around your business, allowing your fans to congregate and interact in a central area. The fans who come to your page will populate this community. There they can share recommendations, memories, testimonials, photos, videos, news, and more. Having them all show up on your Facebook page also gives you a chance to instantly address complaints and customer service or other issues. That's customer relationship management (CRM)—you know, the Second Finger—at its finest and most immediate. To really deepen this engagement with your Kings, I love Facebook Groups.

Facebook Groups are different from regular pages in the way they spark great conversations, not just comments and Likes. That's because the Groups are set up like other web groups, and they have the feel of old-school message boards. Groups can be public or private, which allows us unique ways to use them for e-commerce. Create a private group for your best customers. It's easy to set up a private members-only space where you simply offer information about private deals and links for your elite customers. If you make a Group private, and your customers are forced to ask you for membership, then you know you've got deeply engaged customers. They are committing to being in your sales funnel, and they are more than just circling around the top of it. They are asking you for closer engagement, and they are giving you permission to contact them and market to them. Why else would they do that unless they were interested in buying more products from you?

A Facebook Group Success Story

Just so I can leave the subject of Facebook Groups knowing you have seen success firsthand, here's a little story about how I have used Groups on Facebook.

A client with an online shoe business asked that we build a private group on Facebook for his very best Platinum customers. We built a private VIP Group to show off the new shoes in his inventory to its members *before* making them available to the public. The Group site was also used to host small, interactive events where customers could ask questions and get access through private links to pre-order hot in-demand products.

Creating and crafting unique experiences within Facebook Groups for your customers can really be a blast, and the fun can get your audience super engaged. As a matter of fact, the more fun your Kings are having, and the more special treatment you're offering, the better the Group will be. This shoe company only does its group thing once or twice a month, but when it lets the VIPs know that a private showing is coming up, those folks come religiously. My client has trained this tribe to know that coming to his Group will yield them an experience and a savings that makes it worthwhile to show up. The result has been that several SKUs of shoes, the ones specifically held for these special events, have sold out routinely through the private showings alone. This client never even needed to post this inventory to his site. As these VIP sessions grew, the client eventually moved this whole interaction with his VIP Group onto his own platform. The shoe company grew it on Facebook, and now the owner has it for his own., That means far more control and an even greater personalized shopping experience for his King

Consumers. All this has come from creating a free, private group on Facebook—spectacular!

ICE MAKER

Your Kings' Opinions Become Your New Inventory

My friend Melanie used her Facebook following to pretest and select inventory for her business, Tragic Beautiful. "We would preview designs and ranges [clothing lines] and gauge opinion," she explained. "We would put albums full of images of shoes, and then order the ones that got the most attention. We used Facebook as an almost perfect indicator of buying trends. In return we offered our page fans discounts, special deals, and previews."

Using Facebook this way actually gave Melanie an opportunity to ask which shoes her customers would prefer to buy before she ordered her stock. To her Kings, it seemed just like any other visit to her Facebook page, because Melanie routinely offers images and information about fashion trends. They had no idea that Melanie was actually doing exacting and valuable market research just by asking them to vote for the pictures they liked best!

YOUR FACEBOOK TOOL KIT

As you might have guessed, a platform as robust and powerful as Facebook has some tools you can use to make the platform perform a wide range of tasks you'll need to complete. We're not going to spend too much time or get too techy here with the nuts and bolts of how these tools work. This is a moving target, with new things being developed and offered all the time. Plus, we could spend the rest of the book exploring these tools, but then it wouldn't be a book about social commerce anymore, would it? Instead, I'll concentrate on a few "must-haves" and let you explore them on your own and when you're ready.

Let's take a quick look at some of the tools I like and why I like them.

⬇ ICE MAKER

Stay Informed About What's New for Businesses on Facebook

We'll look at some Facebook tools, of course, but I want to also show you how to stay current with Facebook beyond the time you spend reading this book. Be sure to familiarize yourself with the Facebook for Business section of the site at https://www.facebook.com/business. You can stay up to date on the site's latest tools and developments relevant to your business. I am not going to repeat the Help pages like so many other "experts" do. We're businesspeople, and we're going to get right back to business, which means strategy. I just wanted you to know where to gather all the best resources for staying informed on the platform.

1. Facebook Insights: This tool provides Facebook page owners with metrics about content performance. By understanding and analyzing trends within user growth and demographics, consumption of content and creation of content, page owners and platform developers are better equipped to improve their businesses and create better experiences on Facebook.

2. Simple Facebook Connect: Look guys, I'm all about ease of use and need for speed. This recommendation is *not* for the "official" Facebook version of the WordPress plug-in. Simple Facebook Connect is a secondary tool that I actually believe is better than the one you get through Facebook, and it's described as "a framework and series of subsystems that let you add any sort of Facebook functionality you like to a WordPress blog [which] lets you have an integrated site without a lot of coding that still lets you customize it exactly the way you'd like." You'll find Simple Facebook Connect on the WordPress.org website.

3. Buffer App: This is a supercool tool that allows you to post to your social profile and pages on Facebook, as well as Twitter

and LinkedIn, all at the same time from the same dashboard. It will also track interaction analytics on your Facebook posts and even allow you to schedule future posts and post them over time to your social networks. I really dig Buffer App and use this one every day from my desktop and mobile devices for sharing good content. The free version will allow you to connect one profile for each of the social networks included. If you want more than one, you can pay a fee of $10 per month to have as many as twelve profiles on each network. There is no contract, and you can stop using the paid version and go back to the free one if you find you don't need the extra profiles. You'll find it at BufferApp.com.

4. ShortStack: One of the best-kept cool secrets of success for many e-preneurs, ShortStack has tons of features to help you get the most from your Facebook pages. Among these you'll find contests, polls, data collection, and analytics. Short-Stack offers a free version and paid versions for business that require more functionality. The most popular plan offers enough functionality for most. Go to ShortStack.com for more information.

5. Pagemodo: This site offers some great tools to help you customize your Facebook page for your business. It will allow you to design your cover photo, launch page apps, and more. Pagemodo gives your business a clean and professional social presence in no time, and you'll need no design or technical skills to use it. Using some of the predesigned themes can give your business a professional Facebook presence; engage your visitors with an attractive welcome page. Add photos, maps, and videos at the click of a button. Showcase your products, offer coupons, display your Twitter posts, and much more. You can get a cover page photo and one tab for free! Pricing plans for more tabs and functions are also available at Pagemodo.com.

SUMO LESSON

I met my friend Melanie of Tragic Beautiful (TragicBeautiful. com) in a poker game. She and I were both in Australia for the Professional eCommerce and eBay Sellers (PeSA) Internet Conference, when we found ourselves left among the last few players in a charity tournament. She began her business more than ten years ago as a part-time job that allowed her to pursue her passion, alternative clothing, cosmetics, and accessories. Like many other e-commerce merchants, Melanie ultimately built her business into her full-time job, and today she not only operates one of the largest online sellers of alternative fashions in Australia, but also frequently brings her own designs and creations to her website to list among the other designers. Melanie brought her business to Facebook early in the social commerce game, and she was happy to share some of her early success stories with us.

Melanie had attended a session at the conference that I lead about social commerce and using social media to promote your business. After my second trip to Australia and another conference, I got the following e-mail from Melanie.

Hi John, Melanie from Tragic Beautiful.

We have met a couple of times at Australian conferences—I played poker with you in Sydney at the casino event.

Really enjoyed your talk again. Very motivating and with a lot of practical advice for real things to do rather than vague marketing slogans.

Last year it took me six months but I set up a Facebook page (https://www.facebook.com/tragicbeautifulFB).

When my latest range of clothing came out, I had presold half the order through FB before it even hit my online stores!

Anyway, a big thank you for your presentation and a request to get the PowerPoint slides please. You can e-mail me at info@tragicbeautiful.net.
Thanks!

Mel

After catching up with Melanie, I discovered that although she seems to feel as though she waited six long months to step onto Facebook, it seemed to me she'd been working toward that all along. Sure, she may not have built her presence on Facebook right off the bat, but in the six months between the time she first heard my presentation and the time she was ready to go, she'd spent plenty of time doing exactly what I recommended in the first place. She was listening.

By listening to the conversations and exchanges among her Kings, she was building her background and learning a lot about what they were thinking, doing, and searching for. Once she started with her Facebook presence, she was well ahead of the pack.

Of course, along the way she was also learning other valuable tidbits. She found a lot of success with contests. Melanie and her staff hosted contests on her Facebook page, asking visitors to Like photos or enter competitions. "We obtained thousands of fans overnight due to a photo competition we had," Melanie recalled. "The competitions were fun and even if people didn't want to enter, they loved being able to comment on pictures and select their favorites."

Melanie no longer hosts competitions on her Facebook page. She discontinued them when she realized that people were "buying" votes and rigging contest outcomes. If you noticed, I recommended you host your contests within the invitation-only VIP groups of your Facebook page. That helps you control the nature of the responses.

"I have also learned another very important lesson," Melanie continued. "Never let fans submit anything to your page without it being vetted first." This lesson came to Melanie the hard way. "Thanks to the woman who posted up a series of incredibly raunchy images of herself in a G-string and nothing else on the page, thanking us for great service!" Melanie exclaimed. "We don't even sell G-strings."

But, in spite of a few bumps in the road, Melanie has found Facebook to be a great place to gather among her Kings and share her passion for her products and business. She uses great images, compelling graphics, and frequently changing content to keep her Kings coming back. "By using vibrant, changing and engaging content on our page, we have been able to use our Facebook page as everything from customer support, market research, brand building, relationship building and, most importantly, sales conversions," she said. Interesting. That's every single one of our Five Fingers in one great and dynamic bundle!

That's a Rap!

- ✔ If I have ever polluted my business Facebook page with marketing junk, I won't ever do it again.
- ✔ I recognize that Facebook is a great place to build thrones for my King Consumers.
- ✔ I understand the constantly changing nature of Facebook, and I am building strategies to keep my content fresh.
- ✔ I will use the multidimensional approach to building out my Facebook presence across my inventory.
- ✔ I will use the 80/20 Rule to mix in fun, information, and some calls to action, too.
- ✔ I will provide all the special treatment I can to my Kings both to keep them happy and attract their networks of friends.
- ✔ I will create Facebook Groups to better serve my customers and give them a place to gather and share.

CHAPTER 9

Lights, Camera, Action—You Should Be on **YouTube**

"You can have everything in Life you want, if you will just help other people get what they want."

—Zig Ziglar

love videos, and I love YouTube, because of all its videos. I also love YouTube because it is where I've had some of my biggest success stories while spreading the seeds in my dandelion puff around the world of social media. I've already told you about my bandana video, and now we'll look at that in detail, using it as an example for what can happen when you use videos to spread your dandelion seeds. You'll be amazed at the information you'll be able to gather about your King Consumers, your products, and your social commerce strategies. First, let's take a look at YouTube and how you can effectively use this platform to widen your sales funnel, increase your SEO rankings, gather UGC, build your brand awareness, and give your customers what they need, which is a big part of customer relationship management. Looks like a glove full of Five Fingers, don't you agree?

YouTube is rich soil for you to explore as you scatter your dandelion seeds. According to the site itself, over 1 billion unique visitors land on YouTube each month. That's not considering the ones who come back all throughout the day and use it instead of

TV at night. Those aren't unique viewers, but they are potential Kings with eyes on the platform you're about to occupy. Don't like what you now find on YouTube? Well, give it a second. Every day, seventy-two hours of new video is uploaded to the site, and every month the YouTube audience collectively spends 4 billion hours watching those videos. You can keep up with these ever-expanding numbers on YouTube.

If you're not that into video, you still need to use YouTube as part of your social commerce plan. If you're asking why, I'll answer with a question of my own. What do you think the number two search engine on the web is? Bing ... nah, wrong! Yahoo ... they wish, but wrong again. It's YouTube. If someone is searching online it's likely they're either searching on Google or YouTube. If you spend lots of energy optimizing your content for Google, it does *not* automatically rank on YouTube. But when you optimize content for YouTube, it automatically gets optimized and shown in Google searches, too. It's worth a little extra effort, I'm sure you'll agree.

So, just what is so captivating about YouTube and, even more importantly, video? It's simply moving pictures with words and music, duh! Yep, and that is it! That is what is so intriguing to the masses. It is so *not* rocket science. If a picture is worth a thousand words, then a video is one hundred times more intriguing to us than plain text. I'm going to show you how to take all that human interest in video and turn it toward your business. Our objective? Simply to create videos that will entice, attract, inform, and intrigue your King Consumers.

JOHN'S VIDEO SUCCESS STORY

You already know about my bandana-folding video and how much bang I got for the zero bucks and little bit of time I invested in it. I'll use my bandana video throughout this chapter to share some techniques and tips for making successful videos of your own.

I've had such a huge response to it that all the data it generated can be useful to you as you step off into creating your own videos.

It all began one Saturday afternoon when I decided to put my video camera on a stand, set up a table, and show my customers how to fold a bandana; I was getting so many questions about this, it seemed a quick and easy way to answer a bunch of people all at once. As I write this, that little video has had 275,269 views, which have directly generated 20,821 sales transactions. I traced this data through Google analytics. That's a pretty respectable return for one video that took me less than thirty minutes to make! Not only that, but take a look at Figure 9-1. It's a screenshot of a recent Google search for videos to help the searcher learn how to fold bandanas.

If you type these exact words into Google, "How to fold a bandana," you should see results similar to these, only the numbers will be higher. When I did it today, here's what I found:

Figure 9-1

From 731,000 search results, my video falls on the first page, and it is *above* the fold. It's right there where people will see it without having to scroll down! So anyone who types that phrase into Google's search engine can see my quick and easy video instructions. You'd click that link if you were looking for this information, wouldn't you? How much value would your business get by being listed first on the results page of a Google search? Is it better to be right there near the top? Of course it is. Well, you know I'm not all about hype, and no one can guarantee any one single act on social media will bring you social commerce success, but if you want to increase the chances your business will appear in a Google search result like mine did, your best chance, in many cases, is to use video.

Again, you cannot plan to make a viral video. It just doesn't happen that way. The reality is that you don't need a viral video. You need a video that your King Consumers and their friends will find interesting and useful. The spread of that video will then happen organically, without your having to be the one to spread it around.

As we begin this task together, I'd like you to keep two things in mind that I think both contribute to having success on YouTube:

1. You need to know some of the questions people are asking on any given topic, so you need to keep listening with your social ears.
2. When you answer the question in your video, use the exact words your Kings will most often search with in the video's title.

I admit, I was a bit surprised by my video success, and I'm not promising yours will have the same result. But since I posted this video, I've learned a lot about what makes one video more successful for e-commerce than others, and it involves a lot of details that you can easily duplicate in your business.

YOUTUBE VIDEOS FOR YOUR BUSINESS

Identifying your audience is very important when making videos. Don't be put off by having to create such an exceptional video that everyone will want to see it and share it. That's too much pressure. Instead, focus on making things better for your existing customers. If you make a video that enhances the experience your current customers have with you, *they* will go out and bring you more customers. Here are a few examples of topics to help you get started. "Five Cool Ways You Can Use Product X" or "Three Ways Product X Makes Your Life Easier." These are videos that will enhance your customer's experience with your products or services, and that's more likely than anything else to generate sharing among your Kings' networks.

❄ ICE MAKER

Make Videos for Your Proven Kings

Before you even pick up a camera, phone, or iPad, remember who your audience is. As enticing as it may sound to create dynamic and amazing videos to capture the attention of all those potential Kings out there and bring them to your "door," this is actually not the best way to use YouTube for your business. Make your videos for the Kings you already have within your network. Give them good, usable information about your products, and they'll share the videos. Plus, by serving your existing Kings, you won't be tempted to create a "salesy" type of video, because you've already sold to them. Your goal is to build relationships with your Kings and give them valuable content they'll want to share with their networks.

Since your content is 100 percent relevant to the people who are already buying from you, they'll have reason to share it with others they know who like your stuff, too. And unless you sell something so obscure that only a few people would know about it, your Kings' presence and yours on the Internet's two most popular search engines will also expand your audience to new customers no matter what else you may do. When really, all you're doing is talking to your own customers! Now that's pretty powerful.

But What Should My Videos Be About?

If you've never made videos for your business before, it can seem a little intimidating. First, you want to reduce that anxiety by remembering that YouTube is the home of the amateur video. Nobody expects to see Hollywood production here people, so take a chill and keep some perspective. It's actually pretty easy. Begin by taking a look, once again, at the five or ten most frequently asked questions about your business, and start there. Sit down in front of a camera and simply start answering those questions. If you begin simply, you can focus more on getting comfortable "talking" to the camera, and because you've answered these questions a gazillion times, you don't even have to think too hard to do so. If, in the end, you're just not comfortable in front the camera, find someone who is or do a slideshow using just your voice.

Here are some examples of video topics:

- What types of payment do you accept?
- How are my purchases packaged for shipping?
- What shipping options and delivery times do you offer?
- How can I combine orders to save shipping costs?

Now, will answering any of those questions result in your hitting it big on YouTube? Of course not, but each one you answer with a video could save you from ever personally having to answer it again, and that saves time and ultimately money.

Once you've created your videos, embed their links right into your FAQ pages. Because this content is so highly relevant to your Kings, the videos will get watched, and by the people you want to watch them. A confused customer buys nothing, but a customer who has a question that is quickly, easily, and professionally answered by a human is no longer confused. These videos are guaranteed to increase customer conversion, and you know I don't make those kinds of promises unless I'm really very sure of them.

But that's not all. We all have customers who ask the same questions no matter how well-produced, well-placed, and robust our FAQs pages are. Some people still just need to ask a person. Now, every time you get an e-mail asking about a topic you've got video for, you can respond with a brief but friendly e-mail that contains the link to your video. Not only does this save you time, but it gives your tentative customer a great impression and a personal look at how you treat your customers. You become real to them in ways no e-mail can make you real, and that's great for converting a browser into a buyer. Plus, these videos pay off for infinity! You record a video, upload it once, and it just stays on YouTube without you having to do anything else. The return on investment is astronomical, because the initial investment is just an hour or so of your time.

Educational videos are also fantastic ways to start building your YouTube presence. You know so much about your products that you are an insider when it comes to using them, maintaining them, troubleshooting them, and everything else related to them. Your Kings don't know as much as you do about what you sell, but they know they like it. So, if you can help educate them by teaching them something new about the products they buy, you've got a great source of video content.

Have you ever tried to teach someone something through print? It's hard! It's also very challenging to end up with interesting text someone wants to read. Video works much better for any question with the word "how" in it. Now, all you have to do is turn your camera on and create a video in which you show your customer what he or she wants to know. I think these are some of the easiest videos to make. You can easily demonstrate step-by-step instructions to show your Kings what they need to see. Focus on the task, so the camera disappears a little. The result will be more natural, as though you really were simply showing someone what to do, because that is what you're doing.

So, to answer your question about the content of your videos, make them educational, informational, and relevant to the people who have already proven themselves interested in your work. That's a great place to start your YouTube adventures, and the more videos you make and post, the more ideas will come to you, and the more videos you'll want to make and post!

Make It Easy for Your Kings to Find Your Videos

Once you're ready to go with your videos, you'll need to make sure your King Consumers will find them. Before you set the cameras rolling, think about how you'll optimize these videos in search results. There are basically three main areas you can focus on to make your videos as easy to find as possible.

First, think carefully about the title. Use the keyword you are targeting in the first few words and the last few words of your title. You'll notice if you look back at Figure 9-1 that "bandana" is one of the first words I used when I named my video. (By the way, spelling my keyword "bandana" came from my keyword research. I found that more people used the variant spelling, with only one *n*, instead of using its main spelling with two. I would never have known this if I hadn't taken my time to do my keyword research.)

Your most important keyword should be no more than three words into the title. If you cannot do this, simply use the keyword first, like I did, and follow it with a colon or dash, then add the title. So if your keyword is "camping," but you're demonstrating a hunting knife, then you might title the video, "Camping: How to Clean a Fish with a Hunting Knife."

Remember, not all search results include videos, but you can bet that 90 percent of searches that include "how" in them do. People love using YouTube for the how-to videos. Wouldn't you rather let someone show you how to do something instead of just telling you? So if you search for a how-to video related to your products and don't find one, it's just because no one was smart enough to think of putting one up there. You are, so go for it. Just be sure to put the words "how-to" in the title.

Next, consider your video's description, which appears on YouTube underneath its title. Begin it with the URL of your items landing page, not your home page, but the actual page where people can press the Buy button! Look you've already sold them on the product at this point, so don't make them search around your site to buy it. Let's get this party started on the first click!

✦ ICE MAKER

Use the Fully Qualified URL in Your Description

Hang on a second while I get technical on you. When you post your URL, make sure you use the fully qualified URL. That is, be sure you put the "http://" at the front. YouTube doesn't necessarily need this to make your URL clickable, but this description gets pasted to the embedded code on other sites, and those sites may not automatically identify the URL unless it's the fully qualified one. Not only that, but you also want to be sure every web browser will pick it up and deliver your video as a clickable link. Also, Google has played with how much of the description it will display without you having to hit the More button. Using the qualified URL will ensure that your video ends up driving traffic where you want it to go.

After your URL, be sure to pepper the description with your keywords, not overstuffing them, but including all those that will likely occur to your Kings as they search for information about what you sell. But don't sacrifice good solid product description for keywords. We've got tags for that!

Finally, your tags. Okay, here you can stuff keywords as much as you'd like to. Be sure to include all the other related keywords and key phrases in this area. You don't have to repeat the ones you used in your title or description, so go ahead and add all the relevant ones you can think of.

HOW TO MAKE GREAT VIDEOS

Let's turn our attention to some of the ways you can be sure to offer your King Consumers the best possible videos. Understand that this is fun and creative, not stressful and anxiety producing. You don't have to feel intimidated or self-conscious when you begin, because you're the content expert here. You can do this even if you've never posted a video to YouTube let alone edited a piece of video. Plus, YouTube lends itself to all types of videos, and there's a place for the ones you'll create there, too.

Amateur or Professional?

In my opinion, amateur is the way to go. If you make your video too polished, you run the risk of turning your Kings away, because the result will not feel genuine but more like a sales pitch or commercial instead. YouTube's culture is built on ordinary people uploading things they think are fun or interesting. If you go overboard with production, this savvy crowd of video viewers will spot your pitch in a heartbeat, and then you've lost them. So, that's great news for you! You can stop worrying so much about the final product, because what you can do easily and simply is good enough, and in this case, good enough really is good enough.

I'm not recommending you make really sloppy looking videos. I'm only saying content trumps production on YouTube every single time. Focusing too much on your production will actually defeat your purpose here, so don't go renting special cameras or hiring people who know how to use them, and no special sound equipment, either. You got a camera on your iPad? Use it. You got a camera on the phone in your pocket? Use it. The video you produce will fit right in. If you're not satisfied with the video you get at first, you can always go back and tweak it or reshoot it. Right now, getting your videos done and creating your YouTube channel is way more important.

You Will Need *Some* Equipment

Okay, so we've got the camera part covered, but that's not the only thing to consider. What you may need to buy is some lighting. When making videos about products, you want your viewer to be able to clearly see what you're doing, and properly lighting your set and products will help. Maybe you already have lights that you use when taking photos for your listings, but the ones I like are so inexpensive that you can easily keep them just for video-making. My first video lights were simple clamp lights I bought at Home Depot. I think my total investment was $16.94 for the pair. If you already have a couple of clamp lights hanging around the house, you can save yourself a trip.

I put my two lamps in the room and point them up at the ceiling to brighten the space. The key is that you want to add light to the area you are shooting in. You don't want to shine the lights directly onto the products you are displaying, because then you wash out their details with glare. If your set is well-lit, your video will look great, and your products will be shown in their best light.

How Long Should My Videos Be?

There is a great deal of disagreement about how long your videos should be. Many "experts"—and I use that term lightly—will tell you never post a video longer than five minutes. One of the most powerful and viral videos of 2012 was the thirty-minute piece about Joseph Kony, the brutal rebel leader from Uganda. So, who is right? No one is.

The point of your video is to get right to the point. Don't bother with introductions, product background, blabbity, blah, blah. If you want to demonstrate something about using your product, get started right away. They came for answers to the question "how-to" so get to the meat and show them. If it ends up taking you seven minutes to complete your demonstration, but all seven of them are actually usable and relevant, then your video will be seven minutes. We'll be looking into analytics soon, and we'll revisit this subject of length then, but for now, make your videos clean, to the point, and relevant. We'll worry about timing soon enough.

Edit Your Videos for Clean Results

To get those clean results and keep your videos tight, you're going to need to use some editing software, which can be intimidating to someone who has never worked in video, but it shouldn't be. You'll find some editing tools right on YouTube. As the site has matured, the people at YouTube have recognized the need and answered it with embedded editing features. You can do everything from trimming, to overlays, to adding action items right on the site. That covers the basics. If you find you want more functionality, you do have some commercial choices. I especially like iMovie and Final Cut Pro from Apple. (We'll talk more about them soon.) I use one of these for the more robust stuff I want to do. That doesn't mean you should go right now and buy either one of these. You just don't need the big guns to accomplish simple edits and get professional results. That's possible with the free tools.

I think the iPad camera is superb and it has such an easy interface. I bought an iPad tripod mount for about $30, and now my beloved iPad has become my video camera, and I use it to make almost all my videos. The real value of using it though, is the video apps you can buy in the Apple app store. Apps are a fraction of the cost of the desktop software, and they are much easier to learn and use. With these, my iPad has become my portable photo/video studio. I can take video with it, edit the video, and then upload it to YouTube, Facebook, or wherever I want it to go, right from this one single device. The results are professional and quick. As you know, I like to get to it, get it done, and move on as simply and inexpensively as possible.

Video Meme-Jacking

In the early part of 2013, a little thing called the "Harlem Shake" took off and revived a tired old piece of music, taking it to heights the original song never saw. Before this phenomenon ran its course, the song had reached the top of the charts, knocking down established artists like Bruno Mars, Rihanna, and Drake. All the buzz didn't even start with the original recording artist. What this means is that it became a meme.

A meme is simply anything that goes viral on the Internet. Don't feel too bad if you haven't tapped into the power of memes yet, or even if you don't know how to pronounce the word. I was at a networking event recently when a well-known "Internet Guru" kept referring to it as a "meemay," kind of like something you'd do with the kids on a Saturday morning arts-and-crafts project! It's actually pronounced mēm (rhymes with beam). You've seen them lots of times.

A meme can be a video or a photo or even an expression that has caught on in popular culture. Today the meme gets passed around in various forms on the web. By definition, memes are viral. They're all over the place, sometimes crossing over from online to off-line print and TV ads. They become part of the cultural mix we share with everyone else on the web, and you can use them to your best advantage.

When the Harlem Shake meme took hold, it suddenly seemed everyone—individuals and organizations both—started posting versions of their own dance interpretations of the song. The meme's momentum began to build on February 10, 2013, when the upload rate of versions of the "Harlem Shake" to YouTube was about four thousand a day. On February 11, about twelve thousand versions appeared, garnering more than 44 million unique views. By February 15, about forty thousand videos of the "Harlem Shake" had appeared, totaling 175 million views, in less than a week!

The song went straight to the top of the charts, both domestically in the United States and internationally. That was great news for the artist, Baauer, and his label, Mad Decent records. And instead of worrying about copyright infringement, Baauer and his label made the most of the wild ride. They issued one takedown notice to established artist Azealia Banks when she tried to upload her own version, but they turned everyone else's use of it to their own advantage. They used YouTube's Content ID database to assert copyright over the fan-made videos and claimed a portion of advertising revenue from the site for themselves. That's social commerce at its best!

Now we call the grassroots, bottom-up spread of the Harlem Shake phenomenon a symbiotic viral meme, meaning that culture and business came together. Because a meme is so fleet-ing, traditional advertising agencies or brands can't respond quickly enough to use it. But you, with your quick-and-ready video creation, can. Tie your product to a meme, and you'll be on the way to big SEO benefits.

THE WELL-EXAMINED LIFE OF A YOUTUBE VIDEO

Analyzing data ... I'm not going to lie. I love this part of social commerce. Yes, creating videos is fun, and I love the engagement with my customers, but analyzing the data I get is the best part to me. That's where I can figure out how to make more money. You can, too! Happily, YouTube offers you a robust set of analytic tools built right into the site. These easy-to-use measures give you some very, very powerful information. Look over my shoulder now, and I'll show you what I learned from analyzing the more than one-quarter million views I've gotten from my bandana video. All of these figures represent a period of ninety days of viewership prior to the reports.

The first thing I want you to notice is where people are watch-ing my video. That's where Figure 9-2 helps, because it shows you what devices people were using to see it. I noticed that 49.9 per-cent of viewers used the regular YouTube page from a PC or Mac. Another 43 percent viewed the video on a mobile device. This is fascinating and valuable information, because now that I know mobile viewers are very important, I'll know how important it is to design my videos for the mobile experience, such as making the text on my videos larger than it would have been back when I was formatting it just for the desktop computer.

Shorter videos are probably more likely to get viewed if your King Consumers use a mobile device. I've also noticed from run-ning these analytics routinely that mobile-viewer share is grow-ing monthly. These are signals I need to pay attention to.

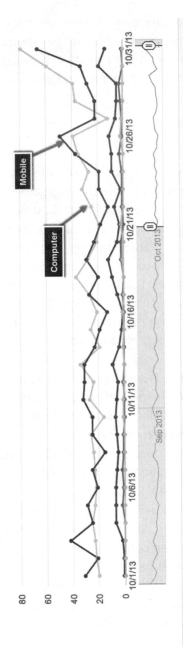

Figure 9-2

Now let's look at the analytic metric that identifies where my Kings are coming from when they view my video. Figure 9-3 shows that 1,969 viewers came from a YouTube search, but an additional 1,213 came from external sites and Google searches. You can see that the YouTube content you create can be indexed in many different places. Below the box in Figure 9-3 you'll see the number 457. Those visits come from having my video embedded in other sites. This is very fascinating to me, because I *never* embedded this video anywhere else. Nope, wasn't me. Nearly 8 percent of my traffic came from the social sharing of others, the ones who are embedding my video on their sites. Some of them are my competitors. Yes, you read that right. My competitors are embedding my video on their sites. Do you think I should make them take it down? *Hell no!* This is the best thing in the world.

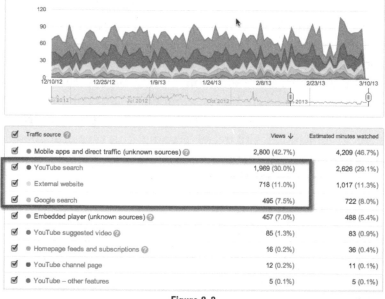

Figure 9-3

153

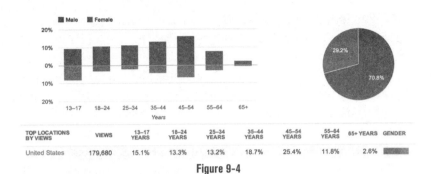

TOP LOCATIONS BY VIEWS	VIEWS	13–17 YEARS	18–24 YEARS	25–34 YEARS	35–44 YEARS	45–54 YEARS	55–64 YEARS	65+ YEARS	GENDER
United States	179,680	15.1%	13.3%	13.2%	18.7%	25.4%	11.8%	2.6%	▬▬

Figure 9-4

Now I'm on their sites and stealing their customers and becoming an authority on this topic. Thanks guys!

Finally, I want to show you how YouTube analytics break down my viewer demographics. I'm only using US viewers for this example. You can see in Figure 9-4 that 64.7 percent of the viewers are male and 58.2 percent are between the ages of thirty-five to sixty-four. Even though I originally made this video intending to reach the younger hip-hop crowd, I see now that more mature viewers are also wearing bandanas and trying to figure out how to fold them. This led me to try and figure out more about this age group and learn what they use bandanas for.

I did a short three-question survey and saw that many of my older viewers were bikers, campers, and scout troop leaders. Now I can tweak my messaging and target this surprising demographic tidbit with my advertising. This type of actionable information is very important when trying to convert the video viewer into a customer!

YOUR YOUTUBE TOOL KIT

To make it simple, I've divided these tools into software that can be used with Mac, PC, and an iPad. You decide which is right for you.

Tools for Mac Users

- iMovie for Mac: This is Apple's popular video authoring tool. With it, you can import video clips from external devices or from anywhere else. Then you can arrange them on a time-line, shuffle them around, and preview the results. When you're happy, you can create a final video file suitable for burning to DVD or uploading to share with others.
- Final Cut Pro: This nonlinear video editing software was developed by Macromedia Inc., and later Apple Inc. The most recent version, Final Cut Pro X, runs on Intel-based Mac OS computers powered by OS version 10.6.8 or later.

A Tool for Windows

- PowerDirector Deluxe: This software offered by CyberLink provides the easiest and fastest way to create and share your videos. With hundreds of editing tools and more than one hundred built-in effects, you can easily turn your videos into something special in no time.

Tools for iPad

- iMovie for iPad: You can make beautiful high-definition movies anywhere with this fast and fun moviemaking app. It puts together everything you need to tell your story, and all that is right at your fingertips.
- Pinnacle Studio: Here's big-screen moviemaking for the touch screen on iPad. This one offers you a great amount of editing technology in an easy-to-use app that will let you quickly edit video, audio, and photos "at the speed of your creativity." You'll find it at PinnacleSys.com.

SUMO LESSON

For this Sumo Lesson, I'm going to let my coauthor, Deb, take the lead.

Okay, John. Hi everyone, I've been here all along, but I wanted to pipe up now with my little YouTube story.

I live in a tiny agricultural town in the foothills of the Blue Ridge Mountains. In town, we have maybe two thousand people, but I wouldn't bet on it being quite that many. The town has been here since before the Revolutionary War, and it's still farming, all the way. Nestled in a pretty little valley, it has been a great place to live for hundreds of years, and people tend to stay here for generations. Having lived here almost twenty years, we figure our family will be natives in another hundred years or so. Anyway, living here is a little like stepping back in time.

Every September, as the harvest season is passing, we have Heritage Day. The county deputies close Main Street, blocking both of our traffic lights! Everyone spills into the street for a parade and party. The parade is a trip! The high-school band plays. We have the entire high-school homecoming court moving in convertibles down the street. There's the coronet band, which has been entertaining since 1892, probably with some of the same members. The local churches all have floats. The scout troops march, the 4-H Club brings animals, and every politician in the county makes an appearance. Everyone throws candy, and the party lasts all day.

One year, my husband decided to post a couple of short videos of the parade on YouTube. I laughed at him. Who on earth would care about our hokey little parade? Well, *shhh*, don't tell him I said so, but he was right! His little clips have more than one thousand views. Plus, there are a couple of dozen other videos posted now, too!

So, what is the business lesson here? Well, there is pretty much an audience for any niche. If you have the content and a good story, you can capture people's attention with a video. I never thought anyone would care about our little parade, but clearly, some do. The lesson I learned was that I need to give more thought to where I can find a deep little market niche that I can fill with my story.

That's a Rap!

✔ YouTube offers me a full fist of support for my Five Fingers.
✔ Making videos is not as stressful as I may have thought it was. I will have some fun with it.
✔ I will target my videos to my existing King Consumers.
✔ I have some great content ideas ready to go.
✔ I will focus on my video's content more than on its production.
✔ I already own enough equipment to get started.
✔ I will study and enjoy analyzing the wealth of data I gain from YouTube analytics.
✔ I will use this actionable information to increase my sales.

CHAPTER 10

Twitter: Lather, Rinse, Retweet

"If you wake up deciding what you want to give versus what you're going to get, you become a more successful person."

—Russell Simmons

Everybody is chirping about Twitter, and I get it. To tell the truth, it's my favorite tool. It's always the right one for me. Twitter's nature is so simple. At the same time, there's a sophistication to its simplicity. There's actually quite a lot of power happening there, so I've found it's easy to underestimate the power beyond this little platform. More than anything, Twitter is *super* simple. Pop onto Twitter, read some quick messages, scan some links, post a link or two of your own, and move on. That's it. The quick and simple way Twitter works makes it perfect for you. Here's your chance to check in and share in quick bursts throughout the day.

For me, Twitter was the lightbulb moment. It showed me the real power of social media. Yes, there was the blog, and you know I think your blog is vital (because I told you it is ... and it really is!), but the deal is, I was really interested in Twitter. And that's because it is very short and quick. Expressing myself in quick bursts is easy for me. I think that way, and I'm sure the entrepreneurs who read this book will agree that ADD is a trait we share. A requirement of being an entrepreneur is to think and move fast. I could take that one little nugget I just found—and I find them all the time—hop onto Twitter, share the URL in fewer than 140 characters, and hop off. Done. I've worked my social network today!

But even better than the quick and easy way I could share what I was doing, was the extraordinary opportunity Twitter gave me to listen in on what other people were doing. I could follow people I did not know. I could follow authors whose books I had read or people I had seen speak at conferences. By following them on Twitter, I could have a look at what they were thinking about and doing throughout the day. Suddenly, I could look over the shoulders of countless people whose work I respected and see what they were paying attention to. What is important to these people? That very simple act of "following" gave me networking opportunities beyond belief. For me, that was a really, really big thing.

I often hear people say, "Facebook is where you go to lie to your friends. Twitter is where you go to be honest with strangers." It's poignant, and I think there's truth in the observation. On Facebook you can create a robust image of your life. It's your life as you choose to represent it in that public space. But because Twitter posts are short, Twitter doesn't lend itself to sharing a lot of detail. It's a pointing tool. You go there to see who is talking about what and what information is getting passed around. Then you share that information with your network, and it's all in the form of short thoughts and tiny URLs.

As I'm sure you know by now, your Twitter comments (tweets) are limited to no more than 140 characters. How did the people behind Twitter come up with that rule? Well, that was pretty simple, too. When the platform was created in the latter part of the last decade, we hadn't yet entered the age of the smartphone. We were still working with flip-phones, and texting was limited to 140 characters. So, there's the big secret behind the magic 140 limit! What we're going to do is look at how you can use those 140 characters—and trust me, you don't need more on Twitter—to reach your social commerce goals in ways that are as simple and powerful as the world of Twitter.

When using Twitter, I especially like to activate the Second, Third, and Fifth Fingers (see Chapter 4). Truth be told, we could actually activate the whole fist with it, but I'm going to show you these three, because I think they give you the biggest bang for your buck. It's hard to beat the immediacy of Twitter for helping you to manage your relationships with your customers, which is the Second Finger. You can respond quickly and directly to any negative comment with an open hand and offer to work out the details directly. Then we'll get to how easy it is for you to share the things your King Consumers are saying about your business, products or services. It's a lot like automatic user generated content, and that's the Third Finger. Finally, as you probably have already figured, Twitter is fantastic for spreading the word about your products, business, and industry, so brand awareness, the Fifth Finger, is a given as you sprinkle Twitter with your thoughtful and interesting tweets. So, let's get started.

❄ ICE MAKER

Shhh! Shhh! Listen to the Tweets

I know you're eager to get onto Twitter and start chirping about your business, but first make Twitter your place to tap into the grapevine and give yourself a continuing and free education. Find a few thought leaders in your industry, and begin following them. Pay attention to what they're thinking and how they're spending their days. What are they interested in? Why are they retweeting the things they retweet? Who among their followers is doing the same? This is the way you find out the buzz in any industry. Within your e-commerce world, you'll find many insights zipping around on Twitter you may never have considered if you hadn't been peeking over the shoulders of those who are driving your industry now. You'll find lots of tweeting going on among your King Consumers, too, so tap into those conversations. Just give yourself plenty of time to listen.

And if you've got a question, add it to the conversation. While you're listening, if there's something you don't understand, ask for clarification. That's still listening, it's just active listening. Just be sure to ask it publicly, don't send it in a private message (PM). Lots of Twitter users ignore PMs because they're often spam. I know I do. You'll begin sharing soon enough. Listening first will give you the right context into which you'll place your content once you start tweeting. We all know what content in context equals ... *ka-ching!*

TWITTER IS YOUR VIRTUAL WATERCOOLER AND A LOT MORE, TOO

Before I started this e-commerce adventure, I was like most of us. I'd worked all my life in an office environment. Sure, working from home for my own business is great, and I love it. But when I started, about ten years ago now, I really missed the camaraderie I'd found at my old office. My coworkers and I bumped into each other throughout the day on errands, coffee runs, or bathroom breaks, and the networking was free and easy. Don't get me wrong, I'm loving life now, but I found when I first left the corporate world, I really had to work to maintain a network of connected business associates.

I tried local business groups, but back then, e-commerce wasn't as prevalent as it is today. A lot of the other businesspeople I met through the usual local channels had trouble actually "getting" what it was that I do. I found the networking lacking, because I wasn't meeting people who really shared my business model and therefore the issues and challenges I was facing. Oh, if only I'd had Twitter back then!

Today, Twitter will allow you to join any type of conversation you may want to participate in. Once you become an active participant, your network will expand as the people who follow you retweet your thoughts to the people who, in turn, follow them, and so forth. Build a following, and you have a direct, two-way line into and out of the world of your King Consumers, the products they use, your competitors they also shop with, the leaders within your industry, and virtually anyone else you may find interesting.

⬇ ICE MAKER

To Have a Friend, Be a Friend

Is there a secret to building a following on Twitter? Absolutely. The fastest way is also the simplest. Follow them first. Mama always said if you want to have a friend, you have to be one, and turns out she was right. That, ladies and gentlemen, is how I got the fifty-seven thousand followers I know are tuned in to me on Twitter as I write this sentence. Follow people in your industry. Use your hashtag (#) keywords for your business that you identified earlier. Search those and find others. Then start following the people who are also interested and tweeting about those keywords.

The ratio of friends and followers who will follow you back is *staggering!* I mean if one in ten or one in fifteen follows you back, now you know your ratio of follow-backs. So if your ratio is one in ten, and you set a goal of having one hundred people follow you on Twitter, then guess how many you have to follow first? 10 × 100 = 1,000. You would need to follow 1,000 people to amass 100 followers. It's simple math, and that makes it all very, very simple. It's true. The fastest way, and in my opinion the best way, to get people engaged with your brand on Twitter is to simply start following them first. You do not want to just wake up tomorrow and follow 1,000 people, that would not be a good way to do it. Twitter is looking out for spammers and might consider your sudden activity a spambot. What you would do is set up a goal to follow 30 or so people per day over the next month. Twitter is a more open form of networking, and the people you follow are most likely to simply follow you back. That is part of the nature of Twitter.

Find Your Choir and Sing Together

Once you have a following, you can start looking for the part of that following that will become your own personal little choir. For example, when I first began tweeting, I talked about e-commerce. I found there were those among my followers who would retweet what I tweeted and share my thought-bursts and links with their own networks. I began gathering a "choir" of followers that resonated. I retweeted them and they retweeted me, spreading my thoughts. My fellow choir members were other e-commerce people. They knew what I was talking about. They understood the lingo and the challenges of e-commerce. They were having the experiences I was having. All of a sudden there were ten people, twenty people, fifty people until, ultimately, at any given time, there were about 56,742 people who followed and interacted with me on Twitter (@ColdICE). Not all at the same time, okay? Let's get that clear.

Do you remember the commercial with Heather Locklear from the '80s? Figure 10-1 shows a still from it. She was talking about Fabergé Organics shampoo, and she loved it. She loved it so much that she "told two friends, and they told two friends, and so on and so on and so on." Every time she said "told two friends" two more little pictures of Heather appeared. The visual image was unmistakable. And this is the type of "spreading the word" I'm talking about here on Twitter.

Let's say I've got 1,000 followers and I have a 10 percent retweet ratio. This means from a network of 1,000 people, 100 of

Figure 10-1

them will find my tweet interesting enough to retweet. Of those 100, each will find 10 within their networks who will retweet, and their friends will retweet, and their friends and, well, you get the idea.

So really, the incredible power of Twitter allows you to first find your choir and then teach them the song and let them sing. And as your choir recruits new members, what will be the first thing you'll do? You'll listen to them. Then you'll use all that you've learned to craft messages aimed directly at your choir, the ones who will take your messages with them as they tweet. And, of course, as you speak directly to your choir, all of your other followers and their networks will be watching, too.

⚡ ICE MAKER

Try Some Klout

If you need a little help finding the people in your industry who seem to be influencing it, try turning to Klout.com. Here you'll find lots of information about many different industries and those who are influencing them. Klout searches across multiple social networks where it can identify influential individuals. You can also use it to track how influential *you* become as you activate your social commerce plan.

Now Make It Personal

Okay, so your network is growing and you've got your choir. Now you can move on to making your tweets and everything else you do on Twitter more personal. People use Twitter to interact with other people. Sure, they follow companies they like, but if you're not Coca-Cola, Southwest Airlines, or Starbucks, then people aren't necessarily going to interact with your brand. What they want is to interact with real people. So, humanizing our Twitter stream has intrinsic value because it allows our followers to interact with us on a much more personal level. That, in turn, makes them want to share what "Paul" just said about this, or what "Donna" just said about that. Anything you can do to make your interactions with your choir, your followers, and your King Consumers seem more human and personal will go a good way toward keeping them engaged and getting them to retweet or take another action you'd like to see.

I learned a lot about this from watching the way the entertainment industry uses Twitter. It used to be that people interacted with *American Idol* or *The Voice* through a single Twitter account. Now each contestant on these shows has an individual Twitter account. So no longer do fans have to be satisfied with following the show in general; they can personally connect with their favorite contestants and interact with those individuals directly.

Granted, you may not have quite as many followers as eager to interact with your staff as with the contestants on these shows, but that's not the point. Let's take the example of Kabbage Inc., the online-financing company based in Atlanta. This company has created Twitter accounts for each of its staff members. Each new employee gets assigned both a company e-mail account and a company Twitter account. Now employees are automatically ready to spread to new areas and gather followings for their company, just like the contestants on TV gather viewers for the shows they appear on.

Fortunately, it's pretty simple to humanize the Twitter experience. If all of your tweets come from YourBusiness. com, followers won't relate to you or feel any real connection. Instead, personally identify the human who created the tweet. You can do this with multiple accounts, or you can sign your tweets with a personal hashtag to make it clear that an individual created it.

Another way you can get your staff involved is to have them use their individual hashtags to identify their posts. This one came from #Barbara or #Becky or #Jimmy. Followers will begin to pay attention and be drawn to these individuals. Why? Because your employees will bring their own personalities to their individual tweets, which will build affinities among your choir for specific members of your staff. People love other people. We're drawn to other people, especially in an environment like Twitter. Of course, let's not forget, your staff will use their personalities to share your business tweets, so make sure they're all properly trained on content matters, or have them send their tweets to you and post them yourself after scanning them. A good tool for that is HootSuite (a little more about this later).

Twitter and the Second Finger: Take Care of Your Customer

Twitter is the perfect environment to interact with your King Consumers and take good care of them. There are many ways to deal with customer relationship issues, but Twitter is the place many of your Kings will come to interact directly with you. And they visit you on Twitter with the expectation that you'll respond. So you must. Once again, keep in mind when you engage a King on Twitter—you are not alone! The entire world is watching you and you need to be mindful of this when you respond to customers. Not only is everyone who follows you watching, but you can assume whatever you do is open for the whole world to see.

If a customer tweets negative comments, it is best to take that discussion off-line and make it private as soon as possible. Of course, the invitation to settle it directly is public, and that's where you'll shine. A polite response I use is simply, "I am very sorry to hear that, please contact (name, e-mail, or number, whatever) for immediate assistance with this issue." *Bam!* Works every time. Now the world knows you are interested, empathetic, professional, and proactive about issues your customers may be having with your products or service. Instantly, you've turned a public negative into a public relations positive.

If you want to test the power of Twitter's customer service response possibilities, just post a tweet about being dissatisfied with your cable company or your phone provider. Almost anyone can relate to being disgruntled with either of those industries at some point. As soon as you can tweet "local cable company X stinks!" you'll get a tweet in response from customer service asking how they may help you. Now they know you'll grumble and complain and that others will join you. They may offer some lame excuse and modest discount to settle it up, and you'll most likely feel exactly the same way about them two weeks from now ... but as an experiment showing the power of Twitter, it's hard to beat.

SOMETHING TO TWEET ABOUT! PUT YOUR CONTENT INTO CONTEXT

Let's bring back that 80/20 Rule I first mentioned in Chapter 8 and discussed in other parts of the book. You're already using it, I expect, and that's good, because there may be no other place where it's more important than it is on Twitter. What I mean is that you're going to have to make sure that at least 80 percent of what you tweet about—what you point people to, what you post— is not about sales. Just like on Facebook, you can't throw sales stuff at your networks as your main communication. If all you post is "here's 10 percent off" and "hey, use this coupon," you're doomed. If you constantly tweet that out to your followers, they'll stop listening to you. They may not bother to stop following you, but they won't pay any attention to your messaging.

Here's what's happening with them. They're not in the mood to shop with you all the time. They like the stuff you sell. They probably share interests with others who also do. Give them content that's interesting to those King Consumers, and you've got it made. You've got their attention. Now they'll remember your 20-percent-off coupon later, down the line, because they're paying attention to what you're doing and saying.

When you post something and find it's really interesting to your choir—you'll know it when they start retweeting it—make sure you tweet that one more than once. Remember, people don't tend to camp out on Twitter. It's interactive, so people check it throughout the day. That means there are all different cycles during which people are on Twitter. You can use analytic tools (and we'll get to those) to find out the best time to tweet things, but don't overlook the off-peak times, too. You might reach a whole different group of people by tweeting then.

This timing strategy is especially great for sharing really big offers or contests. For those tweets, be sure you tweet twice a day. And if you really want to promote something, tweet about it on different days of the week. Suppose you want to promote a contest that will end in a week. That's seven days you have to tweet twice a day, giving you fourteen interactions with your followers. You want to spread those fourteen slots between your peak times and your nonpeak times, sending them out to all parts of your Twitter following.

Get people engaged by asking them to please retweet. Everyone loves a contest or a big sale, so retweeting your offer to their networks will make sense to your followers, too. To make it simple, just add PlzRT to the end of your tweet. Those are probably the five letters that will get your content retweeted the most often. The letters PlzRT will absolutely increase the number of people who will actually retweet, and why? Because you asked. Remember the adage, "You have not, because you ask not." Don't forget, Twitter is a pointing tool, and giving your followers a contest or great sale to point to helps keep them active and engaged members of their own Twitter networks.

⬇ ICE MAKER

Tweak Before You Retweet

So, of course you know, we can't just send fourteen tweets out within the next seven days and expect our followers to still be paying attention—not fourteen identical tweets anyway. So once you decide you have something worthy of multiple tweets, change the tweet a bit each time you post it. This will make it obvious that there's a person behind the tweet and not a software program. Remember, it's people Twitter users want to interact with, so use this strategy to share with a wide range of your followers, but without seeming as though you're a computer trying to blanket the platform with your ads. What I like to do is combine my daily tweets with scheduled prewritten business content. Since I already figured out the fourteen times I have to retweet, I can easily let automated tools tweet out my prewritten business content according to a schedule I set in advance, while adding my daily tweets to the thread more organically.

Make Your Content Count

People in the world of Twitter follow others because they're looking for information and opinions from respected sources. You and the people in your organization often have the deepest knowledge of your products and the lifestyle they support. This knowledge spans broad subject areas, from the materials used in your products to the best ways to use them. Your customer service agents answer the questions all the time. And, all your employees have specialized knowledge in their own areas of expertise. You can leverage this knowledge and demonstrate not only your subject matter authority, but also your commitment to your products and the customers who buy them.

Once again we'll turn to your FAQs. If you took my advice and used your FAQs as the basis for your first blog post, you have the first thing you can point to on Twitter. But before you go pointing away, why not use this opportunity to do some additional King Consumer research, using your Twitter expertise. I'm going to give you step-by-step instructions using my earlier example for the stop-snoring spray in Chapter 4, to show not only how I used Twitter to get involved with a community on behalf of a client, but also how you, too, can benefit from doing this on your own behalf.

The first step is to take a look at the stop-snoring FAQs and identify a few short phrases or questions people use to search information about this product on Twitter. If this is a new product or you still need more ideas about where to start check Wordtracker or Google's keyword tool to see what consumers are searching for when they enter our keywords, "stop snoring."

The next step is to take some of those short phrase questions and put them in the Twitter search box to find the real conversations consumers are actually having about them. I would enter them in the following format: **"stop snoring" -http -www.**

The quotation marks around our key phrase will keep *stop* and *snoring* together during the search. The -http and -www remove all of the tweets with URLs in them from the search. This isolates the search to the questions I am looking for. Go ahead, I'll wait here.

Our immediate results make it clear that, the snorer doesn't do this research. It is the partner who has to sleep with a snorer who is looking for a solution. That insight completely changes how I would recommend that my client write his or her sales copy.

Now I know who to speak to when I craft my responses to help these victims on Twitter and even on my website who simply asked a question and got a huge flood of "noise" in return. Since I know who my client's real Kings are, I can simply begin to answer some of the questions I know they're asking. And with these tweeted answers, my client can now begin to demonstrate authority in this area, and other Twitter users will begin to recognize this authority.

You can use content that already exists on the web to answer some of these questions. Remember the value of Twitter as a pointing tool, and don't hesitate to post tweets pointing to good and reliable information about your products that you found elsewhere on the web. You know your subject area well enough to point these resources out. Pointing a thirsty man to the fountain is almost as good as offering him the water yourself.

The Law of Twitter Reciprocity

The law of reciprocity on Twitter is really just the good old Golden Rule. "Do unto others as you would have others do unto you." Nowhere in the world of social media is this more prevalent than in the world of Twitter. You saw how that works for gaining followers, but it's also true for tweeting and retweeting.

You need to retweet what others tweet and engage in some conversation with your followers. They will do the same in return.

Not everyone, of course, but a percentage of your following will. Since you're working within a specific area of interest, you're bound to come across statements that resonate with you and your business. Show your followers respect by retweeting them, and they'll do the same for your posts. It's part of the culture on Twitter, and you want to be a part of the group, not just a guy or girl who sells stuff.

This is especially effective when you find your followers talking about your products, your service, or things very specific to your industry. Give them a friendly retweet, and you will see a good number of your followers doing the same for you. Twitter users love to get retweeted so this simple act encourages your followers to make comments on your tweets. I make it a practice to retweet and thank any Twitter follower who mentions me or my organization. This lets them know that we are watching and appreciate their mentions. Everybody loves a cool shout-out.

TWEET YOUR VIPS RIGHT

Okay, so remember the story in Chapter 8 about the Las Vegas conference and the VIP line? What I didn't tell you then was that I was in the VIP line because I was a speaker at the conference. This was great since it was a huge conference of about seven hundred people. I was happy not to have to stand in that long "regular" line.

When the start time came, they opened the doors and let all of us in the VIP line go ahead into the club. They had a separate area for us VIPs with its own bar, roped off and everything. Only the VIPs got service at that bar. "The regulars" were not allowed. They really rolled out the red carpet for their VIPs. They succeeded in making us feel special, because we all supported their event.

You can use Twitter to treat your Kings the way I got treated in Las Vegas. Set up a private Twitter account that's just for your VIP Kings and treat them royally. Give them red-carpet access to early arrivals, customer support, or loyalty clubs—whatever! There are many ways to use this more personal and direct communication to create deeper interactions with these, your best customers and cheerleaders. Don't fill this area with information aimed at any old "commoner," like the posts about all your general stuff. Keep this conversation VIP all the way. Keep it red carpet and special, and they will pay attention.

I took one more lesson away from that evening at the Vegas club. Once they let us VIPs in, they started to let in the other guests and partygoers from the regular line. I noticed that the regular folks seemed to enter only in small groups. It's like a few dozen come in and then no more. A little while later a few dozen more come in, and then it stopped again. Mind you, this is a big Vegas club, so why in the world wouldn't everyone in the line have been let in at the same time? I decided to go outside and take a look, because I had some friends who were not VIPs, and I was waiting for them to get in.

I saw right away what was going on. They were using the line in front of the club for marketing! They didn't want the line to disappear. They wanted everyone who went by to see this huge line because, the longer the line, the *more* people want to come in. So people are getting in line to wait to get into this rocking club, while the club down the street with no line can't get anyone to step through its door! Why? Because we as humans want to be where the action is!

What's all of this have to do with Twitter? Twitter is built on constant action. It's hop on, share, hop off. Once you build your following on Twitter, your fan base will emerge from that following. You'll engage your fan base with interesting content they can retweet to their followers, and you'll get more followers.

Plus, this whole time, you'll continue to follow people you find interesting and the people who follow you, too. You're on Twitter to interact, and this much interaction will show people that you are where the action is on Twitter. The more followers you gain, the more people will begin to follow you. It's the law of attraction at work. The line in front of the club has a psychological effect on people. Twitter lets you create that same effect for your Kings. That's a pretty good way to keep the line wrapping around *your* building.

YOUR TWITTER TOOL KIT

As simple as Twitter is—and now you know I wasn't kidding about it being simple—there are still some great tools that will help you get the most out of it. I will recommend a few here, and some of them can be equally useful on other platforms, too. I find them especially helpful here on Twitter, but as we go through these chapters, we're packing your social commerce tool box. Any good set of tools includes the versatile ones you can use in more ways than one.

1. HootSuite: Simply put, HootSuite is the best place to begin with Twitter tools. Go to HootSuite.com to sign up for the free version. This will let you select and manage a total of five accounts on platforms including Twitter, Facebook, LinkedIn, Foursquare, Ping, WordPress, MySpace, and Google Pages. Your free account on HootSuite allows one administrator to control all of your accounts on these platforms. When it comes to monitoring what's going on, you have real power here. You can stream search terms, hashtag feeds, and Twitter lists. You can monitor up to ten streams for each tab you create, and you can have twenty tabs with

your free account. Note: As of this writing, there is currently no good search engine for Facebook. The only thing you can really do effectively with HootSuite there is to monitor the Facebook pages you manage.

2. Social Mention: Here's your place on the web for real-time searches. Your searches are free on the site, and you've got two good options for learning what people are "talking" about. You can search terms across everything, in which case you're searching the "universe." Or, you can select from among more than seventy-five different social networking sites to narrow your scope. Work on strong and precise search terms to get the best results.

3. bitly: Come to bitly.com to create the itty-bitty URLs that make Twitter sharing so easy. Simply copy the real URL of whatever it is you want to share, and plug it into bitly. The result is a "bitmark," a short URL that takes up only a fraction of your 140 characters yet still provides the link. That leaves you more room to comment on that valuable tweet. You can also use bitly to then track and analyze the number of clicks your tweet receives.

4. Topsy: This is another cool tool that gives you the ability to track analytics and break them down by media. That way you can focus on tracking only pictures or only videos. Learn more about it at Topsy.com.

5. Twitonomy: This tool was in beta as I wrote this, but even then ... *wow!* What a cool dashboard to represent your Twitter activity! This is a great graphic representation of everything that is happening with you on Twitter. Check it out at Twitonomy.com.

6. Twitter Counter: Let's not forget the good, old, faithful Twitter speedometer to measure your followers. Just because it's free, automatic, and just because it's always there, doesn't mean it can't provide valuable insights. So use it.

SUMO LESSON

Here's a little lesson that Brad, my coauthor Deb's husband, shared. He's Deb's usual coauthor, and he's spent a lot of time on all the social networks throughout his career. Having spent many years following trends in emerging technologies, he's been an early adopter for lots of great new trends, from telecommuting to e-commerce to social media and more. Brad was a very enthusiastic Twitter user, and he spent a lot of time building a network of followers. Since he lives and breathes the act of gathering information, he frequently posted links to interesting and cool articles about the publishing industry, e-commerce, and a good number of other interests he pursues.

After more than a thousand tweets to many hundreds of followers, Brad's enthusiasm started to flag, because he didn't even know if anyone was reading his tweets. He saw he was getting a few retweets, but not many. He even tried getting his news out early in the day to see if he could become a go-to source for morning headlines among his followers. Without much concrete feedback, he was thinking about ending his Twitter activity and spending his time sharing elsewhere. That's when he happened to a have an exchange with an editor he was working with. He mentioned to his editor that he was a little frustrated with Twitter and was thinking about not really posting much there anymore. The editor responded quickly: "Please don't do that! I always read your posts, and I'd really miss them if you stopped."

Without analytics, which Brad hadn't felt too compelled to use until then, he didn't think his tweets had any particular impact at all. In a random conversation, he quickly learned that, even if he didn't hear back about it, the value of what he was sharing on Twitter was keeping the attention of his followers. Not only that, but just by sharing a bit of his knowledge and personality, he was building trust and respect among colleagues and coworkers. That's a lot of value for a bit of tweeting!

That's a Rap!

✔ I understand that, simple as it is, Twitter is a powerful tool, and I need to learn how to best use it.

✔ I will focus my Twitter activity on the Second, Third, and Fifth Fingers, although I could use it to achieve the other two Fingers, too.

✔ I will follow lots of others on Twitter to gain and build a following of my own.

✔ I know how to tap into the most influential people within my industry, and now I pay attention to what they're saying every day.

✔ I know how to identify my choir on Twitter.

✔ I will address my choir personally and with personality.

✔ I can use Twitter to help with customer service.

✔ I'll treat my VIPs royally on Twitter.

CHAPTER 11

Google+ for Business: The Circle Exposed

"Don't wait. The time will never be just right."

—*Napoleon Hill*

All right. I can see your eyes rolling and hear your groan. Well, maybe I can't actually, but I know what you're thinking: "Why should I worry about Google+? I mean, c'mon. No one uses it." Wow! That is so not true. According to data released in July 2013 by Internet analytics firm GlobalWeb-Index, "Google Plus is racking up large numbers of new users and continues to outpace Twitter as the world's number two social network." That's not exactly, "no one!" Even if I didn't have these impressive traffic statistics to back me up, you'd still have to be on Google+, and I'm not kidding. Still don't believe me? Well then, go Google it!

Yes, that's what I said, and you know it. Google is one of those rare companies with a name that started as a noun and ended up as a verb. Colloquially, people use it to mean searching for anything on the Internet, no matter which search engine they may be using. It's a little like saying, "I'm going to go Xerox this," when you know you're headed toward the Canon copier. Only a few brands manage to make this huge leap from "thing" to "action," but Google managed to do it relatively quickly.

While I can't argue that Google+ didn't get the initial traction that maybe its investors were hoping for, that's got nothing to do with us. Google+ is Google's social networking and identity service. It allows you to connect and share on the web more like the way you connect and share in the real world—in Circles. Since its launch in June 2011, Google+ has continued to add users and is still growing quickly. And get this: Most of these users aren't on Google+ just to link up with family and close friends. They are potential customers on the lookout for reputable and popularly recommended products and services, media professionals who always want to be in the loop with what's up and coming, and even prospective business partners ready to engage in mutually helpful B2B transactions. If you're starting a business or want to push your company to new heights, then you know what this means for you—Google+ may just be the next key to your social commerce success.

So, right from the very beginning, the name "Google" itself made this social network important, but that's where this story gets even better for you. Google launched its social network in stages. When it first came on the scene it was available through invitation only. After several months of populating the site with invitees, Google opened it to the general public. During this early building period, businesses were banned from Google+. The people at Google were concentrating first on getting the platform right before populating it with businesses.

Then Google took social networking in a new direction, from our point of view. It introduced Google+ for Business. This is really the first, and in some ways the *only*, social site that took the initial approach of creating a unique entity specifically for businesses. Google+ for Business allows you to create a corporate account and build a business profile where you can publicly share information about what your company is all about, as well as effectively connect to potential and existing customers through a variety of engaging tools and features. Google+ for Business can help your business boom, and I'm here to show you how.

Then we'll look at some tips and strategies for making Google+ work for your business.

Still skeptical? Okay. Ask yourself the following two "yes-or-no" questions.

1. Would my business be better off if I had a relationship with Google?
2. If I had a relationship with Google, would it be better for my business if they actually took the content that my business produces and married that content to my business, the content creator?

If the answer to both of these questions is "yes," you need to be on Google+. If the answer to even one of these questions is "yes," you need to be on Google+. That's what the site is really all about. Google already indexes every single thing that comes onto the Internet. Now, with Google+, the company is also indexing everything that gets created on the Internet and all the entities that create it. It's indexing the content producers, and when it comes to your business, this means *you!* As soon as the company launched Google+ for Business, I knew it meant the search engine giant was "listening" for business content. Even if nobody else on the face of the earth was listening except Google, you'd still need to be there, so let's get to work on our audience of one.

▼ ICE MAKER

Google Is Listening

Think of that. This company that has become the verb people use to search for things on the Internet, is looking for content that I am producing. It wants to make it easier to find me in Google searches, and it wants to link whatever I create about my business right back to my business. I think this fact requires a little extra consideration, so I'm asking you to actively consider it, just like I've asked you to do lots of things in these little ICE Makers.

We've spent a ton of words discussing all the reasons why you should be listening—to your Kings, to your industry thought leaders, to your competitors—on every platform we've discussed. Now I think you should take some time to consider the power in knowing Google is doing the same thing with you. Gives you something to think about, right?

WHAT CAN YOU EXPECT FROM YOUR NEW GOOGLE PARTNERSHIP?

Now that we've established that Google wants some of the same things we do, let's look at our business objectives to see which of the Five Fingers we can engage through Google+. Well, the Fourth Finger is SEO, which is obviously in play here. Okay, the Third Finger is UGC and Google+ lets your group of followers make recommendations about you with the click of a button. And, of course, we already took care of brand awareness when we agreed that Google would tie our content to our business, giving us ownership of our own content online. But if this near-fistful of fingers weren't enough, Google also offers some tools that will let you both support your customers and communicate with staff and partners easily, directly, and remotely.

I've got to say a word now about Google+ and its Circles. Your network on Google+ is organized by Circles. For the casual user, that's probably the usual stuff—family, coworkers, friends, neighbors, and so on. For a business, those Circles can be whatever you think serves your business best. You could have Circles for different parts of your product line, your vendors, your loyal King Consumers, your business groups. You get the idea. As you add connections on Google+, you'll place each one into a particular Circle or multiple Circles. You can create as many Circles as you want and name them however you see fit. Figure 11-1 shows you what that looks like.

Figure 11-1

183

☆ ICE MAKER

Ask for a Spot in Their Circles

As the holder of a Google+ page for a business, you won't be able to add individual Google+ users to your Circle. They, however, can add you. So, you're going to have to ask them to add you to their Circles. Once they do, you've got them within your Circle, too. Now you can group them according to whatever standards you'd like to apply. You could have them arranged by age, gender, geography, product affinities, or whatever you think is helpful. A Circle created for your very best customers is a good place to send your VIPs direct offers for exclusive events and promotions.

The Fourth Finger: SEO with Your New Partner Google

We all agree search engine optimization is vital to the success of any e-commerce business. Now that you're partners, Google can help you. Google integrates Google+ in the search results it brings up. Now every time someone searches for your brand or company name through Google, your Google+ profile will appear in a box on the right side of the results page. It's highlighted in a big box! It's impossible to look at the search results and miss it. If anyone gets these results and wants to buy what you sell, why wouldn't they just click through and make it that easy? Figure 11-2 shows you just what I mean.

Now, I'm not saying you never have to consider another keyword or update your SEO strategies. We've all been spending too much time and energy in upping the SEO ratings of our websites, and we're likely to keep that up. After all, not everyone searches with Google. I'm only saying that getting your business to appear, in a highlighted box, on the first page of Google search results is great for your business. It's a boost for your SEO ranking, aside from anything else you'll do on social media.

hment

ns, which are
by **Barack**

s the latest

States, the first

ia, Sr.

he American
..

/ Organizing for

os and blogs

this. This page
...

Politico

it **Barack**

the White

ribune

notos and

Figure 11-2

ICE MAKER

Information Worthy of Its First-Page Status

Now that you know a sure way to maximize your SEO ranking, let's revisit the opportunity you have here to completely control your online image. Because your customers are far more likely to see a reference to your Google+ page in a Google search result as their first interaction with you, make sure all your official information and announcements represent your business well. We'll spend more time soon looking at how to create a great profile, but for now, keep in mind what you might want to say about your business when you're ready to build your Google+ presence. Since they're letting you drive, you might as well make the dashboard to your liking!

The Third Finger: UGC, Get a Little Help from Your Friends

We've spent a lot of time looking at how you can engage your King Consumers and then get them to help spread your business messages across the web. By now you know that through Google+ Circles you can create different Circles that will receive targeted messages about specific parts of your product line. But the opportunity to personalize your content to specific Kings isn't the only thing that makes Google+ so valuable, since you can do the same on other platforms.

Google has a "Search plus Your World" feature that makes your messaging more relevant to people who search for your products. On your Google+ business page, you'll find a +1 button. When someone clicks that button, your business profile becomes more relevant, not only to that person, but also to other people in that person's own Google+ circle of contacts. Now, when any one of those contacts searches for a product or service related to your business, your Google+ page becomes more likely to appear in their search results. Google has personalized search results to prioritize pages recommended or "+1'd" by any of the searcher's Google+ contacts. So, in a way, the +1 button can be considered as a sort of personal recommendation online; that is, anyone who clicks it, automatically recommends that page to others, too. Be sure to ask for that +1 from your current friends and followers.

♦ ICE MAKER

+1s All Over the Place

Not only do you get to have the +1 button on your Google+ page, but you can also add it to your own website. These will count to Google also. The more +1s your business accumulates, the better. A count of your +1s will show on your Google+ page, as well as in Google Ads, Google search results, and on your website, once you add the +1 button. The more +1s you gather, the wider your message will reach and so will your solid business reputation.

Make Google+ Count: Put Your Content into Context

Creating your Google+ business page isn't too much different from creating your profiles on the other networks. Still, there are features and strategies specific to Google+, and keeping these in mind will help strengthen your business page with higher, more attractive rankings in search results. We're going to look at the different elements of your page and I'll recommend a few good ways to begin.

Once you and your business page start gathering a following, you'll also want to keep an eye on the stream of messages you post. It's important to understand the opportunities and challenges unique to each platform you choose to occupy, so we'll look at ways you can engage your King Consumers and make that Google+ page work for you.

What Should My Google+ Page Include?

Let's start with your title and description. Your title should be simple here. Use your brand or exact business name. Don't try to keyword-stuff your title; it isn't necessary for Google+. Your title will actually become the name that appears for your business every time you leave a comment on your own or anyone else's posts. Keep it identical to the way you want people to be able to find you.

As for your tagline, well, that can include some keywords, but let's be careful. Your description will appear directly below your title, so make it count. Choose a phrase to describe your business, making sure not to use more than ten words. Include primary keywords here to optimize your page's search ranking, but don't sacrifice meaning or appeal just for the sake of stuffing in a couple more keywords. Craft your description well, because it will likely be the first few words a searcher will read when you pop up on the search results page. I love the one that Zappos has. It is clever ... "We are a service company that happens to sell _____."

Now, let's look at your Introduction/About Page. Here's your chance to shine a bit. Start by deciding what tone you want to take to represent your business. Then you'll know how to craft all your information in that tone. Keep this section informative, but also interesting. If you think it will make your information more readable, and it usually does, include details in bulleted format. Here's your place to put some keywords, but even better, Google lets you apply rich text formatting to emphasize your primary keywords and highlight the main products or services you offer. You can also hyperlink these important words to specific pages on your company website, so your visitors on Google can quickly get the information they may want when they decide they want to know more.

You're going to need a profile picture, and this time it's business all the way. Use this valuable piece of Google real estate for your brand, your business logo, or your storefront. You want this visual to be one your King Consumers will remember, so your brand is way more important than your face is on this platform. In addition to this main photo, you can feature five other photos on scrapbook slots at the top of your page. Choose photos that best illustrate what your business is all about. Take a look at Hugo Boss, NASA, and Starbucks for some inspiration.

❄ ICE MAKER

Rename Those Photos

Before you upload photos to your Google+ page, be sure to rename the files. Give them fitting descriptions based on their subject and content. Here's a place you can include keywords you may have decided not to put into your description.

Finally, be sure to maximize the section of your page that allows you to list recommended links. Order your list according to priority starting with your main company website. Next comes your blog, and finally your business's other social media profiles, such as Facebook, Twitter, and LinkedIn. Organize these entries according to where you are most active and your networks are most engaged. This little tip turns your Google+ page into a portal for people to follow and connect with your business, no matter which social networking site they use most often.

Once They're Encircled, Keep Them There

I know we've been saying that even if the only eyes who occupy your Google+ page belong to Google itself, that's reason enough to be here. But since you already are here, and you've designed your page and linked it to your website and other networks, you might as well keep your Google+ visitors happily encircled with your content. Here are some tips to help you keep their attention, now that you've got it.

Your content needs to be refreshed frequently. Recent posts are more likely to appear higher in search results. Make sure you keep your posts relevant to your Kings' interests, and here's a place for some keywords. Go ahead and include primary keywords in your posts, but only if they appear naturally and are relevant to your subject. Every time you post something, it appears on your followers' Google+ streams, so posting regularly helps keep your business in front of your Kings' eyes. Post new content at least every other day and especially on the weekend when people are most likely to spend time online.

If you're new to Google+, make sure you select the option to share your posts publicly so anyone can view them, even if they're not yet in your Google+ Circle. Have at least ten posts on your page soon after you sign on and continue to post fresh content regularly. You want to attract new visitors to your Circles, but you also want to keep your followers engaged and looking for more.

You can use photos and videos as attention grabbers for your Google+ Circles, and increase the chances of getting +1 hits.

Make your posts interactive by asking your audience questions and encouraging them to respond with comments. This gets them engaged, not only with you but also with the others in your circle. And you should develop good habits of engagement, too. If you get a comment on a post, respond to it. If a follower gives you a +1, thank him for his interest in your business. Remember, Google wanted to create a social network that more closely replicated real human interaction. Making your posts engaging and interactive, remembering to use good manners, and treating your customers like real people instead of just more web traffic are ways you can help your new partner achieve the goals you two signed on for.

GOOGLE+ TOOL KIT

As you might guess, Google added a few valuable tools to Google+. We all know about how many great things you can do on Google, besides search the Internet. You can use some of these tools to support your business and its social commerce goals. For example, Google+ Hangouts will allow you to host ten-way video conferences. That's a pretty effective way to add video conferencing to your business. Couple Google+ Hangouts with Google+ Events and you can host exclusive real-time events that you can invite your special Kings to attend.

Google+ Ripples will take all the public data you've gathered through your public posts or your URL-sharing on Google+ and show you where those postings "rippled" through your Circles. You'll find out who among your network is interested in particular posts, and you'll be likely to discover new members you'd like to follow. Remember, the data you receive through Ripples may not match up exactly with the data you may be gathering yourself, since Ripples only uses public data, so the Ripples count may differ from the numbers you see on the posts themselves.

If you're not sure whether a post is public or private, just look for the word "Public" at the top of the post. If it's there, you're looking at a public post.

You'll find details here about who has publicly shared your post or URL and what comments they made about it. You can see how your post or URL was shared over a period of time, and you can see statistics about how your items are being shared.

You can view Ripples for any public post in your stream just by clicking the down arrow at the top of the post; just click View Ripples. If you want to view the Ripples for a URL, use the Ripples dialog box to enter the URL you want to examine; the visualization should appear. You can share both of these types of Ripples visualization with your stream, if you feel there is something there your Kings may find interesting.

You may also find the following useful:

1. CircleCount: Measure the number of followers within a person's influence on Google+. The higher the number, the more influential that person is on the site. Use this tool to identify interesting people to follow. It will also help you determine how influential your posts and actions are. This tool is at CircleCount.com.

2. Google+ Social Statistics: Not only can you use this to see what is hot and trending on the Google platform, but you can view your own activity in context, too. You'll be able to see who is adding you to their circles, and you'll be able to see your progress over time, too.

3. Timing+: Oh, timing. Everyone is always trying to get it right. Time the market. Time your listings. Time your postings on social media. Luckily, Google makes it easy. Timing+ analyzes your last one hundred posts on Google+ to identify which time seems to be best for you. Just log in through your Google+ account, and all your posts are quantified for you.

SUMO LESSON

I have a friend, Jeff, who writes a lot about careers and job hunting. Of course, in the last five or six years, he's focused a lot on job hunting through social networks. He was invited very early on to join Google+. He did, but he did it out of a sense of obligation. "I figured, what's another profile? I'm on all the others anyway, and this is Google we're talking about," he told me. So, off he went, thinking another apple in the basket, but not much more. He has since told me that he totally underestimated the power of Google+ and its Circles.

"It seems to me that Google was the first one to create a social network with a built-in network management tool," he said. "From the very first person I added to my network, I was asked to think about what he and I shared. Now, I have Circles of contacts that are easy to search, easy to message, and easy to navigate." Sure, the other sites often let you group your contacts and thereby organize your network, but they weren't built with that in mind. Google may have come late to the social networking game, but it stepped in, having identified a valid need, and ready to offer a quick and simple solution.

"I came to realize that I'd allowed myself to grow a little jaded," Jeff confessed. "I thought I'd seen it all and that I was an 'expert' on social networking for jobs and careers. I'd forgotten a lesson I learned long ago, and Google+ reminded me: Stay open to new things. You never know where the next good and useful idea will jump out at you."

That's a Rap!

✔ Now I know that Google, as in giant search engine, is "listening" to my business content.

✔ I've decided that the folks at Google and I share a couple of common goals, so I'm going to partner with them through Google+.

✔ Google+ for Business can dramatically improve my SEO efforts, even if I don't do all the other things I'm already doing to improve it.

✔ I can use Google+ to gather and share UGC, supporting my Third-Finger objectives.

✔ I will use Google+ tools and the public data I can gather to analyze my effectiveness on Google+ and adapt as I need to.

CHAPTER 12

I Meet My Match on LinkedIn

"If knowledge is power then power in business is who you know."

—John Lawson

When it comes to business, who you know really is important. LinkedIn is a powerful network that can make interesting things happen in your professional life. I can't argue that you're likely to see more direct profits and outcomes from some of the other platforms we've looked at, but there's so much value in networking well on LinkedIn, that I wouldn't be doing my job if I didn't show you how I use it and why. Even if everything you ever do on LinkedIn never brings you one single sale, you can still use the site to uncover business opportunities you'd never have known about otherwise and networking connections that, in their own way, can save you thousands of dollars, or more, over the life of your business.

More than 200 million people worldwide use LinkedIn as I write this. There will probably be way, way more when you read it. The people who use LinkedIn are focused on their work and businesses much more than they are in other corners of the social media world. You won't find a lot of off-target conversation on LinkedIn, and virtually none about personal stuff, like kids with the stomach bug or vacation mix-ups we can all laugh about now. People use LinkedIn because they want to share or gain business opportunities and professional expertise. If you're looking for a job, LinkedIn is an obvious choice. But because I'm going to assume most of you are already employed, running your businesses, I'm going to show you how to get great free advice, find business partners, and build your own personal brand awareness—the Fifth Finger, people—all at the same time.

The people on LinkedIn may be more focused on work than those who occupy other social networks, but that's perfect for us because we're using all these social networks for work, too. The culture on LinkedIn expects that you share with the people you connect with there by bringing more to a group or conversation than you take. In this case, the 80/20 Rule says 80 percent of your time on LinkedIn should be spent offering help and advice and 20 percent of your time spent asking for it. This sense of community is one of the things that makes LinkedIn so powerful, and you want to respect it. Just the same, you'll find with your active blogging, and sharing on other networks, offering your LinkedIn community the benefit of your expertise is pretty simple and well worth the effort.

YOUR PROFILE: YOU NEED 100 PERCENT AFTER ALL

Like all the other social networks, LinkedIn makes it easy for you to get up and running on the site. The core of your life on LinkedIn, of course, is your profile. Once you've got that done right, you'll be ready to build your network and make things happen. You won't get much traction on LinkedIn until your profile is 100 percent complete, which basically means completing each element of the profile form, including the addition of a picture and at least three recommendations. I'm not going to hold your hand and take you through the process, which the Help screens describe quite well. Instead, let's spend our time talking about strategy and tips to make your networking time pay off for you.

As you step through building your profile, LinkedIn will keep track of how close you are to that 100 percent. Fortunately, the information you need to complete your profile probably already exists in some form in the marketing materials you've created for yourself and your business. Your task now is to adapt those materials to LinkedIn, and that's simple.

Figure 12-1 shows my LinkedIn profile. Of course, if you check out my profile now, it'll be different, but that's because your LinkedIn profile lives your business life with you and so it frequently changes. This is what I had while I wrote this. I wanted

Figure 12-1

to show it to you, because it illustrates some of the things I think are most important in a profile.

That Photo

The picture you post to your LinkedIn profile sends a specific message. I want my photo to say: Here's John. He knows what he's talking about. You can believe what he says, because he's honest. And just look at that friendly smile. Mama loves me. I think I got that with this picture. Now, you may want to send some of that same message, but you may also want to tweak it to reflect who you are as a businessperson. Be sure that whatever image you choose sends the message you intend. A headshot that shows you looking professional but friendly and open is the place to start.

This is all a part of building your overall professional and business brand. Make sure your photo only includes you. It's not the time to include a partner or your employees. Save that for other sites. This profile is yours and should be focused only on you. Don't stress too much about what you wear. If your business persona is more formal, then go for it. If it means something more open like mine, then that's fine. Your LinkedIn photo is valuable space, so make it work for you.

⬇ ICE MAKER

Change Your Photo

Now that you know what your photo should look like, you need to change it up. That means that at least twice a year, you should switch out whatever profile photo you're using for another one. That's not so your network can see your new hairdo or your latest pair of glasses. It's way more practical than that. If you leave it static, then the people who view your profile will just start to ignore it. You know how humans are. Regain their attention by switching it up every now and again.

Tips and Tricks for a Great Profile

Next to your picture is your headline. It's okay to list yourself as CEO of your company, because you are. I also mention I'm a social commerce strategist, because that's an important part of my business. If you wear more than one hat, separate your different job titles by a slash (/). It makes each one stand out more and reads well on a screen.

When you first signed on to LinkedIn, its computers randomly assigned a URL to your profile page. Be sure, if you haven't already done it, that you go in and edit that. You want your LinkedIn URL to be exactly the name people would use to search for you. Right under my picture is my URL, www.linkedin.com/in/colderice. Nobody forgets colderice. When people decide to look me up after one of my speaking engagements, I want it to be easy for them to find me. Colderice does that for me. The good news is that LinkedIn profiles rank very well in search results, so if someone wants to find you, this little trick will make it much easier. That's the Fourth Finger, people, good old SEO back in the game.

Below the picture in my profile, you'll see a window that shows my activity. This is going to reflect everything I do online, because I'm linking everything I do on my blog to all my social networks, including LinkedIn. Keep your activity fresh and changing. Make it something people within your network will want to read, comment on, and repost. Your dandelion seeds will keep on spreading.

I told you I wasn't going to walk you through every aspect of building your profile, and I'm not. I do want to take a quick look at the summary area, because this is a corner of the profile that people often misuse. It's not just a quick summary of your resume, so you shouldn't use it that way. It's a part of your profile that lives and breathes as you work every day. Make it an ongoing description of your achievements and the problems you've solved. Be sure to show people not only what you've done but also what you are doing, and are capable of doing for others in your network and beyond.

THINGS I DO ON LINKEDIN: IF IT DON'T MAKE DOLLARS, IT DON'T MAKE SENSE

As you know, this book is all about making money; the "commerce" part of the phrase social commerce. A good friend of mine once told me, "If it don't make dollars, it don't make sense." If I don't see a benefit that results in more money, I have to direct my energies toward something else.

I'm going to share with you some of the ways I like to use LinkedIn to meet my own business objectives. As someone who operates a growing e-commerce business, I have all the same issues that you do: finding reasonable and reliable vendors, vetting potential business partners, hiring virtual workers, or even the in-person ones. I've also found that LinkedIn is a great way to learn about upcoming conferences and meetings to preplan how to use your travel dollars wisely.

Participate in Groups

There are more than 15 million groups on LinkedIn. You'll find a group for just about any industry you can name. When you join a LinkedIn group, all the members who already belong to that group become part of your network in that you can contact them directly. Members within groups engage each other in discussions, share news and data relevant to the group, and ask and answer questions. When you search for groups that might be interesting, take notice of how many members belong and how active the discussions are. You want to spend your time where people are actively engaged and sharing.

With more than 15 million choices, I clearly can't leave you to wander around trying to decide which ones you should start with. Exploring the Groups feature on your own will open up new opportunities—especially once you find the groups that are most specifically aimed at people within your industry—but just for now, let's get you started with some of the ones I find to be useful.

John-Approved LinkedIn Groups

1. Kick Ass Social Commerce Group: This group was created specifically for you guys—the ones who read this book. Here's where you can ask questions, talk about ideas, and communicate with other members. Of course, I'll be there hanging out, too.
2. eMarketing Association Network: With more than half a million members, you'd be crazy to miss the chance to tap into all that experience. The group is managed by the eMarketing Association; you can find details here about its annual conference.
3. Ecommerce and Online Marketing Experts: Discussions within this group include topics as diverse as finding good communications software, maximizing profits from an eBay store, and the results of studies about e-commerce and the practicalities of creating videos. You get the idea.
4. Social Commerce: Selling with Social Media: This group has nearly three thousand members who share their knowledge and experience. You'll find technical discussions and advice and lots of data about trends in social marketing and networking.
5. eBay Sellers: Official eBay Group: You guessed it. Everything to do with eBay is here, from the latest eBay changes to feedback issues to dealing with eBay corporate. You know how eBay people love to talk, so count on lots of opinions.

Find and Vet New Vendors

Everyone who operates a business needs to build a network of reliable vendors to fulfill the demand for any number of different products and services. Online merchants always have a nose out for the next great inventory addition, but there are all kinds of vendors who can help you keep things moving along, and LinkedIn Groups can help you find them, connect with them, and vet them. Join the groups you think will be most helpful to you and your business, and then search the discussions to see what others recommend in terms of finding and vetting vendors. You can always start a discussion of your own if you don't find one that addresses your specific question. Just remember to answer other peoples' questions when you can. Be a friend, make a friend.

Once you have some prospective vendors to consider, do a company search on LinkedIn to see not only how they represent themselves professionally, but also what current and former employees have to say about them. That's where most of the company information on LinkedIn comes from, making it insider knowledge, which can definitely give you a richer and deeper picture of what a company is truly like than all the PR material you could collect.

LinkedIn Today, a Nose for News

LinkedIn Today is your own custom RSS news feed right on LinkedIn. Rich Site Summary, aka Real Simple Syndication or RSS, of course, is nothing new. You set your RSS feed on whichever browser you use, and then every day, or however often you choose, you'll get a custom delivery of news relevant to the search terms you chose. It's an old tool, but LinkedIn Today brings it up to date by showing you the news stories people within your network, groups, and industries are sharing. It's a very easy way to get the "buzz" of what others in your corner of the social media world are talking about.

Use Your Travel Dollars Wisely

There is no denying the power of meeting people face-to-face. Going to a conference or a trade show where you can mingle with your peers is the best way of all to cement the relationships you build through e-mail and social media. At these meetings you can find new vendors or attend seminar sessions that address issues you might be facing in your business. Plus, I never leave a conference or trade show without something new to think about based on what I've seen. They are very stimulating places to be. Still, in good economies and bad, there is only so much money set aside for business travel, education, and networking.

I use LinkedIn to identify which conferences and shows I'll attend. Set a calendar for yourself and decide how much travel you can afford, both financially and in terms of time away from your business. Then you can decide what you hope to gain from going to each conference or show and build your strategy around those goals. A quick search of LinkedIn Groups for the term "e-commerce conferences" found several articles that discussed the e-commerce conference calendar for the upcoming calendar year. There were ongoing discussions of which shows were most productive and travel details, too. The same search for trade shows brought up more than two hundred entries for both domestic and international shows. If you make your travel decisions early in the year, you are also more likely to save something on travel and hotel expenses, so that's money in your pocket, too.

SUMO LESSON

LinkedIn is personable, and we want to keep it personable. Part of that requires everyone to really interact with the individuals who connect with them there. This can be difficult to do as your network grows. How do you manage to interact personally with so many people? Well, of course, being in touch routinely with that many individuals is probably a bit unlikely. But even if you have say, 200, 300, or even 500 people in your network, it's still possible to be personal with enough of them to keep LinkedIn person-to-person, and show your personal touch to your network and beyond. I like to use the Recommendations feature to do that.

When you write a LinkedIn recommendation for a person in your network, it shows up both on that person's profile page and on your own. Both of your networks get notified, and that puts your name out there among your crowd. The good thing about randomly sprinkling unsolicited recommendations among your network is that it builds your place as a member of the group. Those in your LinkedIn network will see that you take the time to give to individuals who invest their time and attention by being part of your network. Plus, people are really responsive to being recommended on LinkedIn. Just think, on a random day, out of nowhere, you reached out and said, "Good job." It's bound to brighten anyone's day. So, several times a week I offer unsolicited recommendations to people in my network.

Like so many other instances in social media, the best way to get recommendations is to give them. But trading recommendations on the site, one in exchange for another, is easy to spot on LinkedIn and savvy LinkedIn users frown on it. If you send out unsolicited recommendations, some of those people will respond in kind, but some won't. It'll look more randomly generated than the prearranged ones do.

Be sure to select your keywords carefully when you craft your recommendation to make it easier to find during searches. Don't go overboard by adding a couple of dozen keywords. It's not necessary and the list is going to get boiled down to the top two or three anyway. So just select the top few and use them. It'll get you a better return.

That's a Rap!

✔ My LinkedIn profile is 100 percent complete.
✔ My blog activity shows up on my LinkedIn profile.
✔ I changed my personal LinkedIn URL to make it easy for people to find me.
✔ I know the message my photo is sending and I approve.
✔ I've joined a few groups, both John-recommended and those I discovered on my own.
✔ I will remember to give more to the LinkedIn community than I take.

CHAPTER 13

Put That Pin Down and Say Cheese: **Pinterest** and **Instagram**

"I'm not afraid of dying. I'm afraid of not trying."

—Jay Z

H ere, in the very last chapter of this book, we'll spend some time exploring the two most prominent photo content sites in the social media world: Pinterest and Instagram. Relative newcomers to social networking, these two sites represent an incredible repository of visual content. Tap into their potential, and you can help spread your brand, your products, and yourself all over the web. If you're selling goods online, then you know how important great photos are to your business. You are most likely spending a lot of time, money, and effort to provide your King Consumers with good quality photos of your products. That's been drummed into your head from the very first listing you posted and with good reason.

We humans are visual creatures. Although we surely don't have eyes as sharp as a hawk's or an eagle's—and in low light, even our house cats fare better than we do—we still gather an enormous amount of information with our eyes. As a matter of fact, 90 percent of the information we take in comes to our brains through our eyes, reported Amanda Sibley on HubSpot in the summer of 2012. Couple this with the fact that King Consumers are now far more interested in finding their products online rather than searching for them, and we can't overlook the importance of these two sites specifically designed to collect your images. Luckily, you can add both of them to your social commerce mix simply and efficiently. Before we get started, let's first look at some of the reasons online merchants consider using Pinterest and Instagram.

1. Because everyone else says it's a good idea, and they are doing it.
2. They heard about it at an event and everyone was talking about how these sites are beating even Facebook.
3. Because they know their competition has a presence there.

Wrong, wrong, and wrong again. C'mon people, the only reason to use these sites is because they fall in line with our social commerce strategies, and because they can help us work better, stronger, and faster. That's the focus we'll take as we explore visual content marketing. The good news is that Pinterest and Instagram are so simple to use, that if you're not already on the site—and judging from the number of new users, you probably are—you'll find yourself up and running in no time. I'm going to focus on some very specific ways you can use them both to reach your goals.

Before we start, you should first decide what you want your pictures to represent about you, your brands, and your business. We'll look at some specific things you can do to gain exposure through these platforms in just a bit, but as with all things in social commerce, spend some time thinking about what you want to achieve before you just start posting your photos. I've said it before, but it still bears repeating: Setting your objectives and then planning how to achieve them will be your keys to success.

PINTEREST

Simply put, Pinterest is an online bulletin board. Pinterest users sign up using their Facebook, Twitter, or e-mail accounts. Once signed into the service, you can create boards to house all the cool visuals you come across as you surf the web. Sign up and you'll get a Pinterest button that resides on your browser's toolbar. Find a picture you like, and with the click of that button, you've posted it to one of any number of Pinterest boards you're free to create. You can then gather followers and follow others, too.

Pinterest is clearly here to stay. In 2012 the site had the most growth, year over year, of any social media site. In December 2012, Nielsen's 2012 Social Media report pegged the jump at 1,047 percent in unique PC visits and mobile usage grew by 1,698 percent. For the most part, more women use Pinterest. The Pew Research Center reports they are five times as likely to be on the site as men. The Center also reports that Pinterest users trend toward the younger demographic, with the majority falling between the ages of eighteen to forty-nine. As you can see, a lot of your Kings are likely to fall into these categories. So, how can you make the best use of Pinterest? Well, let's start with the fact that you're not going to go there to actually sell anything. You're going to use Pinterest instead to share with your Kings and get them to share with you and each other, too.

Five Ways to Use Pinterest Now

1. Post only the original picture: You will grab more attention and interest if your pictures are unique.
2. Do unto others: Do your business a favor by helping others. You can win other people's hearts by endorsing their content on your boards. You follow them, and they're likely to follow you back. This way, you will be able to build up a wider level of followers. Just be sure that the content you

---

choose to repin and share is somewhat related to your products and services.

3. Create useful and attractive catalogues: Use a mix of both personal and business photos. If the pictures show images of your actual products, don't hesitate to put the price along with a brief description with the picture. That way, your followers know exactly what your intentions are. By being clear about your intention to sell, interested buyers can be clear about their intention to buy. You can actually pin your catalogue from your website, and then your followers can navigate the whole thing.

4. Host a competition: The most logical contest to host is a photo competition. Have your followers post their pictures and then choose the best among them. Reward the winner with recognition on your board and a prize from your inventory. Also be sure that you leverage your user generated content from all the entries.

5. Ask your followers to be involved: If they're following you, then they share an interest in your products. It's safe to assume they'd be willing to share your good reputation with their networks. Never overlook the power of word-of-mouth promotion. It's still a great way to spread the word about your business.

INSTAGRAM

Instagram is the picture-sharing site of the mobile world. We all know how important mobile is, not just for today, but from now on, too. So, Instagram is a must, if you plan to share pictures. It's become nearly impossible to find a mobile device today that doesn't include a camera, and a pretty good camera at that. People can go through their days snapping images of every little thing that suits their fancies. With Instagram, you can immediately share those images with your friends, family, and really the entire world of other people who are also snapping pictures and sharing them.

❄ ICE MAKER

What's in a Name? Plenty!

When you use your phone to take and post pictures, whether to Pinterest or Instagram, be sure to rename them. Your camera will automatically add a generic name and description to your image, something along the lines of "123.jpg" or "cam123.jpg." By creating an original title and description for each image, you'll make it easier for people to find them. Search engines can't "see" your photos, and these randomly assigned names don't mean anything. With good titles and descriptions for your images, you give search engines the terms they need to index your photos; SEO, the Fourth Finger.

The good news is that sharing images through Instagram is as easy as pushing a button. Instagram is available for iPhone, iPad, and Android devices. The Instagram app itself is free and available through both the Apple App store and the Google Play store. As of this writing, Instagram had just enabled web viewing via your PC or notebook, but the web presence for these devices is limited only to viewing your Instagram account. You still have to do all your navigation through your mobile device, which is fine, since that's also the way your consumers will navigate it, too.

For the most part, those consumers are more likely to be women than men, and they're also likely to be younger than fifty years old, according to the Pew Research Center. African-American and Latino users overindex in the category of Instagram use. The Pew study shows 23 percent of African-American and 18 percent of Latino-American internet users are on Instagram, while only 11 percent of Whites use the platform, and users overall are more likely to live in urban areas rather than rural, according to the Center. If this is your target demographic, you will find they're using Instagram as their own version of Twitter. That's all the more reason you should be on Instagram where they hang out.

Five Ways to Use Instagram Now

1. Set Instagram as your default app for photo sharing. You do not have to worry about your old Facebook or Twitter account for your business, since it is very easy to share your Instagram photos through these social networking giants. That's a big time-saver.
2. Search your hashtags to determine your most popular brands. Then you can look at other posts relating to your company and brands. Once you find these you can ride on the trend and sustain it. Allowing others to help you by promoting your business is so important, because self-advertising is not something Instagram users appreciate.
3. Unlike other platforms at the time of this writing, such as Facebook and Google+, Instagram doesn't allow for separate accounts for your business and personal use. It does not reserve a separate classification for brands. Your Instagram account for your business will look just like everyone's personal account.
4. Make sure each photo you upload places your products and your brand into a larger context. Each of your photos should say something significant about what you do and sell. Since you know your photos are "speaking" to your consumers, make sure they're actually saying something worthwhile.
5. Once again, host promotions and events within your community of followers. This will get you much greater exposure within the group and that can easily be converted into increased sales and profits.

CAPTIVATING IMAGES YOU CAN BEGIN USING—AND I MEAN NOW

Now that you're up and running on Pinterest and Instagram, I'm going to offer you a couple of quick and easy ways to add great content to your photo collections and get them moving. This whole system works best if your followers pick up what you post and spread it through their networks, just like the bees and the flowers in my overgrown yard. If you want them to do that, you have to inform, entertain, and delight them a bit. Using infographics and meme-jacking are two ways I like to make that happen.

Infographics

Infographics is simply information presented in a visual and graphic way. This first became the rage when the people at *USA Today* introduced it in the 1980s. They wanted a new, easily digestible, and visual way to present information. Infographics are attractive, often colorful and, although they are fun to look at, they actually convey very usable information. Now, if you're clever with graphic design, you can create your own infographics. But, for the rest of us, there's no need to do that. You'll find scores of them on the web already, created by people who are very happy to have you repin them or share them with your network on Instagram.

Let's use the example of an e-commerce merchant selling pet supplies. Simply go to your search engine and enter a search for "pet infographics." When I did this search, I had more than a million responses in subjects that ranged from "How much does it cost to own a pet?" to "How to care for your dog in the summer heat," and "Which pet is right for me?" Now you have a choice of what you're going to pin on your Pinterest board and share on Instagram. Every time someone searches for these terms, you're boards will be part of the search results. You're not advertising your products, but you are sharing information with your consumers, and that's the way into your King Consumers' hearts.

Photo Meme-Jacking

Think of that picture of Gene Wilder's Willy Wonka saying something smart-assed. Photo memes are all over the place. Although they originate on the Internet, they sometimes also cross over from online to the offline world of print and TV ads. They become part of the cultural mix we share with everyone else on the web. So, the good news is, if you meme-jack one of them, your brand and your products will go with that meme, and your dandelion seeds will find fertile ground where they can plant your brand. You'll be surprised how easy it is to do this.

The first thing you want to do is identify a meme that will work for you. If you don't recognize one just through the time you spend online, you can find them easily enough. I like two super easy meme generators: Meme Generator and Quickmeme. Either one will provide you with enough visuals to begin with. So let's look at our pet-supply dealer and see how he's meme-jacking. Figure 13-1 shows the image he created to go along with the caption "50 Shades of Grey." Notice Leo's Pet Care and his logo up in the left corner. You're likely to get a chuckle when you come across this, and if you have pets, you might just decide to click through to the site and see what's for sale. Either way, Leo's meme will be part of the search results every time someone searches for this popular and racy title.

 Leo's Pet Care added a new photo.

Like · Comment · Share · 15 seconds ago ·

Figure 13-1

SUMO LESSON

Not too long ago I was in a radio station for an appearance on a talk show, hosted by Brent Leary. I happened to have taken my fifteen-year-old sister with me that day. She wanted to see how it all worked. The show's topic was about new social-media sharing platforms. Earlier that week, Amazon had experienced an outage on its service that brought down both Instagram and Netflix. Brent asked my little sister, live on the radio, which social networking site she uses to keep up with her friends. "I use Instagram," she said. I had no idea until that moment how important the site was to her. In her world, Instagram is Twitter. I was surprised, and on live radio!

As we part ways, I think that's an important lesson: The world of social media, and so the world of social commerce, is constantly changing. You are starting out on an adventure that will require you to keep working in the present but looking toward the future. There are always more King Consumers coming of age, and the younger ones will use social networking sites in ways we may not yet be able to imagine. So, go out, pay attention, have some fun, and kick some ass!

That's a Rap!

✔ I will get a Pinterest and Instagram account ready to go.

✔ I am considering which of my images I want to use first.

✔ I will pay attention to my titles and descriptions to help with SEO.

✔ I will provide usable information to my consumers, so they will share it.

✔ I've found a few infographics I'd like to use.

✔ I'm going to meme-jack something cool by the end of the week.

Acknowledgments

Big shout-outs and thanks to my husband, John, without whom this endeavor would not have been possible. Thank you, Babe. Thanks to my wonderful family who are so supportive of me. And to Mom and Dad, who raised a kid with their examples of stick-to-it-iveness and love for education. I had the best parents I could ask for, really.

Thanks to Phil Leahy, the first person on earth to put me on stage with a mic, because he thought I really had something worthy to say. He gave me a platform and the courage to say it in front of thousands. Thanks to my fellow Original Kings of Technology (#OKOT) buddies with an extra special shout to Brent Leary for all these years of breakfast brainstorming over coffee, and to JB when he could get a "hall pass." My coauthor, Debra, and her husband, Brad, you guys believed it from the start and you are the binding that holds this book together. Thanks for your guidance and wisdom.

Huge shout-out to my e-commerce "partner in time," Jon Miller, who has put up with my bullshit for three years waiting for this book to be birthed. Big thanks to the ColderICE team: Karen, Michelle, and Jacqui, unparalleled support ladies. To all my friends and followers in social media and the members of the Facebook Ecommerce Group; dude, you guys are the reason why I am here and why the publisher took a chance on a guy like me ... *Thank you*. Thank you, thank you, and thank you! You guys freakin' rock my world, and I luv y'all!

I want to thank my agent, Bill Gladstone, and the staff at Waterside Productions for taking this idea and finding it a great home ... which leads to my publishing team. Thanks to the folks at BenBella Books, who put this book into your hands. Glenn Yeffeth, the publisher, believed in it. Thank you, Debbie Harmsen, Editor-in-Chief, and Monica Lowry, in charge of the art. Thank you to Leigh Camp and Jessika Rieck, who saw this manuscript through production. Thanks to my copy editor, Francesca Drago, who caught all my mistakes, and my proofreaders Greg Teague and Rainbow Graphics who double-checked for me. A special thanks to Erin Kelley, who answered all my questions quickly and with such good cheer. You all made a big project much, much better!

What's up to the OG ColderICE Squad: Bryan, Randy, Kat, Jason, Mel, Danni, Janelle, Deb, Lynn, Joe, Scott, Mark, Beth, Brandon, Kathy, eBay Andy, Ms. Jazzy Love Jam, Cliff, Pineapple, Lisa, Uncle Joe, Shaun from down under, R.B.H., "Marsha, Marsha, Marsha," Phaedra, and Wally.

And to my "kids," Elijah, Jasmine, Deva ... The world lies, always try. Love you guys.

—JL

I'd like to thank my coauthor, John, for letting me live inside his brilliant head for these past months. He always argues with me about the "brilliant" part, but trust me. I've been inside that head, and there's no other word for it, well, except maybe genius. I started this project with a business associate, but I end it with a lifelong friend. Thanks, John.

I'd also like to thank everyone at the C. Burr Artz Public Library for putting up with my being away from work and distracted by this amazing book. That's especially true for my "family" in the Children's department. They picked up extra story times when I wasn't there and took on extra work so I could be free to write. I will bring you cupcakes, I promise.

To my family, starting with my husband, Brad, there are not enough thanks in the universe. You are still, as you always will be, the Sweetheart of My Youth. Also thank you to my kids, Stephanie, Andrew, Ethan, and Laurel. Watching you four write your own life stories is the joy of my existence.

—DS

About the Authors

Mixergy calls **John Lawson** a "power seller." American Express hawks him as their "featured businessman." Startup Nation says he's the "savviest" in Social Media and Small Biz Trends named him "Influencer" of the year. He is an award-winning Social Media Strategist, a spokesperson for several corporations, a commercial television personality and a sought after Keynote Speaker, Trainer/Instructor and conference panelist.

John is also the founder of ColderIce Media, an eCommerce education, training and consultant agency headquartered in Atlanta, Georgia, and 3rd Power Outlet his online clothing business has executed more than 350,000 online transactions resulting in more than $25 million dollars in sales.

His easy humor, combined with his concrete knowledge and expertise in Social Business and eCommerce, has put him in front of tens of thousands of businessmen and women around the world. He has traveled to nearly a dozen countries to teach would be millionaires how to achieve their internet business goals. His ability to convey complex concepts in an understandable language has made him "the toast of the town" on the Social Media speaking circuit.

As editor of the industry leading ColderICE.com blog, John dispenses his down-to-earth wisdom in a matter-of-fact manner that charms and enthralls his audiences. He's not merely a talking head. John has proven that he is the 'real deal' when it comes to knowing how to navigate the intricacies of the Internet and in teaching others how to successfully do what he has already done.

Debra Schepp is the author of 19 books, including *How to Find a Job on LinkedIn, Facebook, Twitter, and Google+*; *eBay Power-Seller Secrets*; and *How to Make Money with YouTube*.

The first edition of her LinkedIn book resulted in her being honored by the National Press Club at the 32nd Annual and Book Fair and Authors' Night. The *Washington Post* named her YouTube book among the top 10 business books of the year. She has been interviewed many times by national media including *LIFE Magazine, Forbes,* and *Entrepreneur* magazine. She has also appeared on many radio shows and her work has been featured in publications such as *Newsweek,* the *Chicago Tribune, Parade,* and *LIFE* magazine.

As a former editor for McGraw-Hill and Gartner Group, she has been writing about living and working online since the 1980s! This is her first collaboration with John. She lives in rural Maryland with her usual coauthor, husband Brad.

Index